AUNT DAN
AND LEMON

A PLAY BY

WALLACE SHAWN

DRAMATISTS
PLAY SERVICE
INC.

AUNT DAN AND LEMON
Copyright © 1986, Wallace Shawn
Copyright © 1985, Wallace Shawn

All Rights Reserved

CAUTION: Professionals and amateurs are hereby warned that performance of
AUNT DAN AND LEMON is subject to a royalty. It is fully protected under the
copyright laws of the United States of America, and of all countries covered by the
International Copyright Union (including the Dominion of Canada and the rest
of the British Commonwealth), and of all countries covered by the Pan-American
Copyright Convention, the Universal Copyright Convention, the Berne
Convention, and of all countries with which the United States has reciprocal
copyright relations. All rights, including professional/amateur stage rights, motion
picture, recitation, lecturing, public reading, radio broadcasting, television, video
or sound recording, all other forms of mechanical or electronic reproduction, such
as CD-ROM, CD-I, DVD, information storage and retrieval systems and
photocopying, and the rights of translation into foreign languages, are strictly
reserved. Particular emphasis is placed upon the matter of readings, permission for
which must be secured from the Author's agent in writing.

The stage performance rights in AUNT DAN AND LEMON (other than first
class rights) are controlled exclusively by DRAMATISTS PLAY SERVICE, INC.,
440 Park Avenue South, New York, NY 10016. No professional or non-
professional performance of the Play (excluding first class professional
performance) may be given without obtaining in advance the written permission
of DRAMATISTS PLAY SERVICE, INC., and paying the requisite fee.

Inquiries concerning all other rights should be addressed to Rosenstone/Wender,
3 East 48th Street, 4th Floor, New York, NY 10017. Attn: Howard Rosenstone.

SPECIAL NOTE
Anyone receiving permission to produce AUNT DAN AND LEMON is required
to give credit to the Author as sole and exclusive Author of the Play on the title
page of all programs distributed in connection with performances of the Play and
in all instances in which the title of the Play appears for purposes of advertising,
publicizing or otherwise exploiting the Play and/or a production thereof. The
name of the Author must appear on a separate line, in which no other name
appears, immediately beneath the title and in size of type equal to 50% of the size
of the largest, most prominent letter used for the title of the Play. No person, firm,
or entity may receive credit larger or more prominent than that accorded the Author.

Dear Deb, this is for you

NOTES IN JUSTIFICATION OF PUTTING THE
AUDIENCE THROUGH A DIFFICULT EVENING

We all know how enjoyable it is to see a film about the nineteenth century in which sadistic and greedy slave-owners, dressed in comical costumes, sit on the porch of a mansion and breezily philosophize, justifying their vile way of life with ludicrous and insincere rationalizations. And there's even something somewhat gratifying, one has to admit, about seeing Hitler in a newsreel, with his silly mustache and silly haircut, screaming hysterically and shaking his fist. And one of the reasons we like to see such films or such newsreels is that they give us the reassuring feeling, as we watch them, that we're the sort of people who can recognize evil when it presents itself—the sort of people who will recognize it and immediately reject it if it ever should approach us. The people in the film about the nineteenth century may be fooling each other, but they don't fool us. We can easily see that their arguments are false. And even when we watch the newsreel, although Hitler is trying his best to impress us, he fails completely. We see right through him, and we utterly despise him.

Unfortunately, it does little good to those who were murdered by Hitler in the 1940's that we look at newsreels of Hitler today and see him as a hideous monstrosity. What doomed those people to a horrifying death was the fact that the audience that was listening to Hitler's speeches at the time he was actually making them found him very compelling. Hitler's mustache style, unfashionable today, was seen by the people of the time as quite attractive. The passion in his speeches seemed heart-felt and honest. The accusations he made about the injustices committed against the German nation by the Treaty of Versailles were very persuasive. And the people who listened to Hitler's speeches had often heard that he was fond of children, and fond of his dog.

Watching too many newsreels from the distant past, too many films about the nineteenth century, can give us a feeling of over-confidence. It would be flattering to believe that we are superior in some way to the audiences who cheered for Hitler—more insightful and perceptive, let's say, or less bloodthirsty—but I think it would be more prudent to make the assumption that perhaps we're not. At least we should allow ourselves to imagine that possibility for just a moment. After all, if we do turn out to be superior — if we are, in fact, a uniquely benign and harmless group of people, blessed with unusual clarity of vision — then our moment of over-cautiousness will have cost us nothing. Whereas if it should happen to turn out that we're *not* superior, our self-examination might save a lot of people — possibly all people — from being harmed by us.

It was difficult for the people who listened to Hitler to see him as clearly as we do today. They didn't know about the crimes he would ultimately commit. And the Treaty of Versailles really was unjust. Much of what he said about it was absolutely true. Hitler's personality had some warm elements that were attractive to people. And from what I've read, I'm prepared to believe that he did love his dog.

Now there are people who will argue, No, he could not have loved his dog. There was nothing good or attractive about him, nothing true in what he said. And in my opinion the reason they make that argument is that if Hitler did *not* love his dog, if he did *not* ever say anything true, then we know that we all could have seen him for the monster he was. As soon as we admit that he *might* have loved his dog, then we begin to worry that perhaps we would *not* have seen how evil he was, perhaps we're *not* superior to the people who listened to his speeches all those many years ago, perhaps we too might have been confused, perhaps, in fact, we're confused right now. We lose our certainty that the people we admire now are not evil, that the arguments we believe in now, the things we say and the thoughts we think, are not evil, and we ourselves are not evil.

A play presents a self-enclosed little world for the audience to examine. It's an opportunity to look objectively at a group of people, to assess them, to react to them, and to measure oneself against them, to ask, "Am I like that?" Every playwright tries to present on stage — in the world he creates — something like an aspect of his own view of the real world, the world outside the play, and as I find the real world to be disturbingly complicated and hard to figure out, I've written a play in which it's hard to say whether you like some of the people or you don't like them, and in which the things people say are a complex jumble of lies, truth, half-truth, rationality, and irrationality — in other words, things in the play are just the way things seem to me every day when I read the newspaper or talk to friends, colleagues, and acquaintances on the telephone. In the world of the play, evil triumphs, whereas my own view about the way things stand in the real world is that we might still be able to prevent the complete triumph of evil, particularly if we recognize that the complete triumph of evil really is a possibility and that the partial triumph of evil has already occurred.

Intellectual clarity seems to me a very important weapon in the fight against evil, although "clarity" is of course a very difficult concept to define. I think staying awake rather than falling asleep when people are talking to you is an important component of the definition of clarity, and I think theatre can give people a certain training or practice in this type of vigilance. It's really quite simple, in a way — actually listening to what people are saying, actually watching what they're doing, and then judging what you've heard and seen by your own standards. It's simple to describe, but it's actually quite hard to do, and theatre can help us to learn how to do it.

Lemon, in AUNT DAN AND LEMON, doesn't say the same things Aunt Dan has said, and you, in the real world, don't say the same things Lemon has said. Lemon's attitudes are different from Aunt Dan's in certain ways and different from yours in certain ways. But there are also similarities. Is Lemon a bad disciple of Aunt Dan or a good disciple? Is Lemon a million miles away from you, or me, or is she somewhat closer?

Lemon's thoughts have unlimited destructive power. I didn't invent them — they're everywhere. If thoughts already existed which in their force and mass could decisively defeat Lemon's thoughts, then Lemon's thoughts would already have been defeated, whereas in fact they're gaining ground. Perhaps I could have defeated Lemon's thoughts in the confines of the play, but this would have given the audience the impression that in my opinion those thoughts had been safely buried at least for the evening and everyone could go home and sleep in peace, whereas actually I don't believe that. I actually believe that we all have to figure out how to defeat these thoughts, whether I defeat them in the play or not, and so in fact to defeat them in the play and give the play a satisfying ending would be, for me, a form of lying to the audience.

Besides, to demonstrate the vileness or illogicality or falseness of Lemon's thoughts or reasoning, or anyone's thoughts or reasoning, wouldn't tell you what to do about the questions that have been raised about how we should live in the world. If these questions are easily answered, then each person can easily provide his own "satisfying ending" to the play by answering them for himself. If they're hard to answer—as I find them to be—then each person can add his strength to the common struggle to answer them.

I *have* wondered, in case anyone's interested, What gives *me* the right to ask these questions? What gives me the right even to *think* about such things, to write about such things? I'm not a victim, a survivor. I haven't suffered. I'm not even a scholar, a statesman, or a professional student of international affairs. How can I—a superficial American, nurtured in the citadel of privilege, sheltered from the winds of history, a writer for the theatre whose life consists of brunches and telephone conversations, of hours spent lazily exchanging views on Nicaragua and the latest theatrical openings with actors and mimes—how can I even mention such subjects, which should rightly be approached with awe and humility by those who are truly worthy of them, who have earned the right to speak about them? My conclusion—after wondering for a while about this question—was that *anyone* has the right to think or speak about them, because it's in fact impossible to say in advance whose contribution might be of value—just as it's impossible to predict which of the twelve jurors in a jury trial will, in the course of that jury's deliberations, point out some crucial bit of evidence that no one else has noticed (because it often turns out to be the person who gives every outward indication of being the least clever, the least perceptive)—and there's a time factor, a need to understand these subjects quickly, now, so it makes sense for everyone to leap in immediately and start to think. We still haven't even come close to understanding what happened in Europe in the 1940's, and how much less do we understand what's happening now, what may happen tomorrow. What's important, of course, from the world's point of view, is not

7

what's in our heads, but that our behavior should change—our behavior and the attitudes which underlie it—but how can we start to change our attitudes or our behavior if we haven't first thought about why we must change and in what direction?

Wallace Shawn
April, 1986

The world premiere of *Aunt Dan and Lemon* was produced by The New York Shakespeare Festival (Joseph Papp, Producer) at the Royal Court Theatre, London, England, August 27, 1985, with the following cast (in order of appearance):

LEMON .... *Kathryn Pogson*
MOTHER .... *Linda Bassett*
FATHER .... *Wallace Shawn*
AUNT DAN .... *Linda Hunt*
MINDY .... *Lynsey Baxter*
ANDY .... *Larry Pine*
FREDDIE .... *Wallace Shawn*
MARTY .... *Larry Pine*
RAIMONDO .... *Mario Arrambide*
FLORA .... *Linda Bassett*
JUNE .... *Linda Bassett*
JASPER .... *Wallace Shawn*

This production was directed by Max Stafford-Clark; set designed by Peter Hartwell; costumes by Jennifer Cook; lighting by Andy Phillips and Christopher Toulmin; sound by John Del Nero and Andy Pink; stage managers, Peter Gilbert, Jill MacFarlane, and Bethe Ward. The assistant director was Simon Curtis.

The New York production opened at the Public Theater on October 21, 1985.

AUNT DAN AND LEMON

NOTE: The action of this play is continuous. There should be no pauses at all, except where indicated, despite the fact that the setting changes.

London. A dark room. A woman named Lemon, born in 1960. She sits in an armchair, weak and sick.

LEMON. Hello, dear audience, dear good people who have taken yourselves out for a special treat, a night at the theater. Hello, little children. How sweet you are, how innocent. If everyone were just like you, perhaps the world would be nice again, perhaps we all would be happy again. (*Pause.*) Dear people, come inside into my little flat, and I'll tell you everything about my life. (*Pause.*) Maybe you're wondering about all these glasses, all these drinks? They're all sweet fruit and vegetable juices, my friends. I spend all my money on these wonderful drinks—lime and celery and lemon and grape—because I'm a very sick girl, and these juices are almost all I can take to sustain this poor little body of mine. Bread and juices, and rolls, of course. (*Pause.*) I've always had a problem with regular meals— I mean, regular food at regular hours. Maybe it's only a psychological problem, but it's destroyed my body all the same. (*Pause.*) My parents both died in their early fifties, and it wouldn't surprise me if I were to die even younger than that. It wouldn't surprise me, and it wouldn't bother me. My father was an American who lived most of his life over here, in England. He worked very hard at his job, and he made some money, which I inherited, but it's very, very little with today's prices. It allows me to live, but not much more. (*Pause.*) Maybe because I have nothing to do all day, I sleep very little, and I make a lot of effort just trying to sleep. I used to read mysteries—detective novels—to put myself to sleep, but I don't any more. Lately I've been reading about the Nazi killing of the Jews instead. There

11

are a lot of books about the Nazi death camps. I was reading one last night about the camp called Treblinka. In Treblinka, according to the book, they had these special sheds where the children and women undressed and had their hair taken off, and then they had a sort of narrow outdoor passageway, lined by fences, that led from these sheds all the way out to the gas chambers, and they called that passageway the Road to Heaven. And when the children and women were undressing in the sheds, the guards addressed them quite politely, and what the guards said was that they were going to be taken outside for a shower and disinfection—which happens to be a phrase you read so often in these books, again and again, "a shower and disinfection." "A shower and disinfection." The guards told them that they didn't need to be worried about their clothes at all, because very soon they would be coming back to this very same room, and no one would touch their clothes in the meanwhile. But then once the women and children stepped out of the sheds onto the Road to Heaven, there were other guards waiting for them, and those guards used whips, and the women and children were made to run rapidly down the road and all the way into the chambers, which were tiled with orange and white tiles and looked like showers, but which were really killing chambers. And then the doors would be slammed shut, and the poison would be pumped in until everyone was dead, twenty minutes later, or half an hour later. So apparently the Nazis had learned that it was possible to keep everyone calm and orderly when they were inside the sheds, but that as soon as they found themselves outside, naked, in that narrow passageway, they instinctively knew what was happening to them, and so guards were stationed there with whips to reduce the confusion to a sort of minimum. The strategy was to deal with them politely for as long as possible, and then to use whips when politeness no longer sufficed. Today, of course, the Nazis are considered dunces, because they lost the war, but it has to be said that they managed to accomplish a great deal of what they wanted to do. They were certainly successful against the Jews. (*Pause.*) The simple truth about my life is that I spend an awful lot of time in this room just doing nothing, or looking at the wall. I can't stand the noise of television or even the radio. I don't have visitors, I don't do crossword puzzles, I don't follow sports, and I don't follow the news. I hate reading the daily papers, and actually people who *do* read them in a way seem like idiots to me, because they get wildly excited about every new person or thing that comes along, and they think that the world is about to enormously improve, and then a year later they're shocked to learn that that new thing or that new person that was going to make everything wonderful all of a sudden was in fact just nothing or he was just a crook like everyone else, which is exactly what I would probably have guessed already. So the fact is that I spend a lot of time just staring into space. And you know, when you do that, all of your memories come right back to you, and each day you remember a bit more about them. Of course I haven't lived much of a life, and I would never say I had. Most of my "sex," if you can call it that, has been with myself. And so many of my experiences have had to do with being sick, like visiting different doctors, falling down on my face in public buildings, throwing up in hallways in strange places, and things like that. So in a way I'm sitting here living in the past, and I don't really have much of a past to live in. And also, of course, I should say that I'm not a brilliant person, and I've never claimed to be one. And actually most of the people I've known as an adult haven't been that brilliant either, which happens to suit me fine, because I don't have the energy to deal with anybody brilliant today. But it means that I'm really thrown back on my childhood, because my most intense memories really go back to my childhood, but not so much to things that I did: instead I remember things I was told. And one of the times that was most intense for me — and that I've been thinking about especially in the last few days — is a certain summer I want to tell you about. And to describe that summer I have to tell you a little about my background and go a bit farther back into things. And you know, people talk about life as if the only things that matter are your own experiences, the things *you* saw or the things *you* did or the things that happened to *you*. But you see, to me that's not true. It's not true at all. To me what matters really is the people you knew, the things you learned from them, the things that influenced you deeply and made you what you are. So I may not have done very much in my life. And yet I really feel I've had a *great* life, because of what I've learned from the people I knew. (*Lemon drinks. A long silence.*

13

Very faintly in the darkness three seated figures begin to be visible.) How far do your memories go back? Mine start when I was three: A lawn. The sun. Mother. Father. And Aunt Dan. (*The seated figures stand and form another picture. Mother and Father have their arms around each other. Aunt Dan is slightly apart.*) Then a little later, sort of at twilight, everyone walking, then suddenly stopping to look at the sky. Mother. Father. And Aunt Dan. (*Mother points at something in the sky. Father and Aunt Dan look.*) And then there are the things that happened to other people, but they're mine now. They're my memories. (*Raimondo, a Hispanic man in his forties, and Mindy, an English woman in her twenties, are seated at a table. Music in the background.*)

RAIMONDO. (*To Mindy.*) What absolutely wonderful music — really delightful —

MINDY. Yes — isn't it?

RAIMONDO. It reminds me of — er — Brasilia Chantelle — do you know that group?

MINDY. No —

RAIMONDO. They have a vibraphone, a banjo, a sax, and a harp. Not your ordinary combo — eh? (*They laugh.*)

MINDY. You seem to know a lot about music, Mr. Lopez.

RAIMONDO. Well, music is one of my passions, you see — you know, I'm afraid I didn't catch your last name.

MINDY. Er — Gatti.

RAIMONDO. Italian?

MINDY. On my father's side Italian. My mother was English.

RAIMONDO. She's no longer living?

MINDY. Yes — she died last winter. A terrible illness.

RAIMONDO. I'm very sorry.

MINDY. Oh, thank you, really. Do you like this wine?

RAIMONDO. It's delicious. It's special.

MINDY. Yes, it's Italian. — The sparkling wines of that region are always —

RAIMONDO. You picked it?

MINDY. Yes.

RAIMONDO. You like wine, don't you?

MINDY. Not *too* much, no —

RAIMONDO. I didn't say *too* much —

MINDY. You were thinking it, though — You were thinking I look like the kind of person —

14

RAIMONDO. *Every* person is that kind of person. I'm a student of the subject. Ha ha! Believe me. But I like it, too. When a wine is good—and the company's amusing—

MINDY. When the company's amusing, *any* wine is good. (*They laugh. These figures fade. June, an English woman in her twenties, Jasper, an American man in his forties, and Andy, an American man in his early thirties, are now visible, seated in the midst of a conversation.*)

ANDY. (*To June.*) Tell us your opinion.

JUNE. Jasper seems to me an attractive man. He's extremely polite, he's extremely friendly. I'd be very surprised if he had any diseases—diseases, Jasper?

JASPER. Absolutely not. Do you think this kind of thing is my normal life? I *never* do this. I'm on vacation. (*These figures fade, as Lemon speaks.*)

LEMON. (*To the audience.*) But to tell you about myself, I have to tell you something about my father. I can't avoid it. And the first thing he'd want me to tell you about him is that he loved England. That's what he always said. He came here first to study at Oxford, and then he met my mother, an English girl. And then, when they were married, they decided to live in England for good, and Father got a job in a huge company that made parts for cars. Jack and Susie. My father and mother. (*Pause.*) But poor Father always felt that his old friends, the people he'd known when he was a student at Oxford, had no understanding of the work he did. He would always tell us they didn't have a clue. He used to say that over and over and over again. (*Father smiles at the audience, finally speaks.*)

FATHER. I love England. It's a beautiful place. The gardens are lovely. Those English roses. The way they have strawberry jam and that clotted cream with their high teas. And crumpets particularly are very wonderful, I think. There's no American equivalent to crumpets at all—the way they seem to absorb butter like some living creature—the way they get richer and richer as you add all that butter. Well, you can't get anything like that in America at all. But you know, it's interesting that there are some fantastic misconceptions about English life, and one of them is the amazing idea that economic life in England is somehow relaxed—not very intense! Well! Ha! When I hear that, I have a big reaction, I have to tell you. And when I tell people about economic life in England today, the first thing I say is, it's *very* intense. It's *very* intense. You see, the first fact to know about economic life in England today is that it's very, very hard to get a really good job over here. And the second thing that people just don't seem to know is that if you *have* a good job, it is very, very hard to keep *hold* of it. Because people don't realize that if you *have* a good job, then to *keep* that job, you have to *perform*. You really have to *perform*! If you're on the executive level, you have to perform. You do your job right, you get the results, or out you go, I don't care what school you went to, my friend — that stuff about the schools doesn't count any more — you can just forget it! The thing is now, they look at the figures: Are the orders up? Great. You're okay. Are they down? Believe me, you're out, my friend. I always say, if you don't think I'm right, try sitting in my office for just one week. You'll know what I'm talking about then, you see. That's just what I say to all my old friends when they ask me about it, in that somewhat awkward way that they have. They're all academics, they're scholars, they're writers — they think *they're* using their brains every day, and *I'm* somehow using — ? — well, what? — my feet? And that's why I say, I wish you would sit in my office for just one week and do my job and then see whether you need your brains to do it or not. Well, maybe you're so smart you won't *need* your brains — I really don't know. Maybe I'm stupid! But just try it out. Try it for a week and give me a report. Those lazy bastards would drop to their knees with exhaustion after a single day of the work I do. Because the amazing thing about the work *I* do is that you don't just do your work and then say to yourself, "Well done, my boy. That was very well done!" You see, that's what scholars do. That's what writers do. And if you're a scholar or a writer — great — fine — no one in the world can say, "No, No, but your work was bad." Or they can say it, maybe, but then *you* can say, "Oh no, you're wrong, it really was good." But in *my* work there's an actual test, a very simple test which tells you without any doubt or question or debate at all whether your work was in fact "good," or whether it was, in fact, very very "bad" — And the test is, how did your product do in the market? Did people buy it? Well, your work was good. What? They didn't? Well, I'm very, very sorry, your work

16

was *bad*. It was *very bad*. You did a *bad job*. You see, it's no good saying, "But the public doesn't understand me, in twenty years they'll know I was right." Because in twenty years the product won't be on the shelves, you see, so it will be perfectly irrelevant in twenty years. In twenty years that product will be out of date—it will be worthless garbage. So the judgment that's passed on the work I do is extremely harsh, and the punishment for doing badly is very simple: you have to leave. So at the executive level, you can't relax. You work hard. You work hard, you pay attention, and the next day you go in and you work hard again and pay attention again. And if you miss a day—if you go in one day and you just don't feel like working hard, and you just don't feel like paying attention—well, that could very well be the day when you make the mistake that costs you your job, the whole thing. I've seen it happen to a lot of people. I've seen it happen about a thousand times.

LEMON. Some people have warm memories of their family table. I can't say I do! There was a problem about that family table for me. (*At the dinner table, Mother, Father, and Lemon are silent. Mother and Father eat. Lemon just plays with her food.*)

MOTHER. What's wrong, my love?

LEMON. Mummy, it's raw.

MOTHER. That lamb?—Raw?—But it's *overcooked*, darling—I was trying—please—I wanted—

LEMON. I'm sorry, Mummy.

MOTHER. But you have to eat—if you don't eat—please—I can't stand this—

LEMON. May I be excused? (*She leaves the table, but stands nearby, where her parents can't see her. To the audience.*) Father was sure that my problem was caused by the very anxiety which my mother expressed when I didn't eat. (*She eavesdrops on her parents' conversation.*)

FATHER. Susie. Susie. I know how you feel! I know how you feel! But you've got to get yourself under control! Yes, it's a *terrible, terrible situation*—but *you're causing* it!

MOTHER. Oh no—please—

FATHER. Yes! Yes! I am right about this! I am right about this! You've got to get yourself under control! Because if you don't, we're going to have a really sick girl around here! And I

17

mean *really sick*! Do you hear what I'm saying? I mean it, I mean it! If you don't get yourself under control, we're going to have a really sick girl, and doctors will have to come here and *take her away*. And I mean *far away*. For a *long time*. So control your feelings! When she *leaves* this room, you can cry, you can scream — and I'll cry too, I'll cry right along with you — but when she's *in* the room, you *keep quiet*! We're dealing here with a sick child, a helpless child, *she* can't help feeling *sick*! Don't you *know* that? She would like to be well! She would like to be well!

MOTHER. Love — please — you   mustn't — don't — darling — you're becoming —

FATHER. No. You leave me alone. You leave me alone right now. Don't you start telling me what I'm becoming. Don't you dare. I'm not nothing. Don't you say that I'm nothing. Don't you ever *dare* say to me that I'm nothing.

LEMON. (*To the audience.*) I listened in the way that children listen. I didn't actually hear the points they were making, point for point. It was more of a sound I heard. There was a certain sort of sound she made, and a certain sort of sound from him. My mother was a saint — she loved him very dearly. But my father was a kind of caged animal, he'd been deprived of everything that would keep him healthy. His life was unsanitary in every way. His entire environment — his cage . . . was unclean. He was never given a thorough washing. So no wonder . . . his fur was falling out, he was growing thinner and thinner every day. His teeth were rotten, his shit was rotten, and of course he stank. He stank to hell. When we sat at the table, as if everything was normal, everything was fine, there was an overpowering stench that was coming from my father. My mother ignored it, but you have to say, she did get sick and die at the age of fifty. (*Lemon, as a young child, is in bed. Mother is talking to her.*)

MOTHER. I loved the dawn at Oxford. I loved the way my room looked when I would draw the curtain, and that little bit of gray light would come in and spill over my books. I loved the way the books looked in that dim light — dusty, cold, delicious. I remember there was a whole winter when every morning I got up at dawn, brushed my teeth, made myself a big pot of coffee, and then sat down at my desk, which was right by the window, and I wouldn't get up until it was almost noon. And I remember that sometimes when I would stand up after so many hours of reading poetry — it was the English poetry of the seventeenth century — I would be giddy and unsteady on my feet until I had rushed to my cupboard and eaten a hard-boiled egg and a bun and a big square of chocolate, all in about a minute and a half. And then I would go out, and that same winter I'd discovered this huge meadow near the edge of town where I used to take walks. And one afternoon as I walked along I saw another girl who was walking also, and as I was looking at her, she looked over at me. And then a few days later, I saw her again, and we found ourselves staring at each other. Finally it happened again a few days later, and the other girl decided to introduce herself. She marched up with a sort of mischievous grin, extended her hand, and announced in a forthright American accent, "My name's Danielle." And you know, Dan in those days used to wear these delicate white Victorian blouses and these rough nineteenth-century men's caps, and I'd never met anyone quite like her in my life. So we walked together for a little while, and then I said to her, "Well why don't you come back to my room for tea?" And so we went back, and we talked for a very long time, and we drank a lot of tea and got very excited, and we drank some sherry that I'd put away somewhere, and I told her things I hadn't told people whom I'd known for years. I was shocked at first when she said she was a tutor, but I quickly got used to it, and a week or so later she came back again, and then she came once again. And a few weeks later she brought one of her friends — another American — and it was your father, of course.

LEMON. My parents had named me Leonora, but when I was very little Aunt Dan started calling me Lemon, and then I called myself that, and it became my name. And when I was still very little, five or six or seven or eight, I remember how close Aunt Dan and my parents were. (*Mother, Father, Aunt Dan, and Lemon are at the table.*)

AUNT DAN. Dear God, thank you for this meal we are about to eat. Thank you for this table, thank you for these knives and forks and spoons and these plates and glasses, thank you for giving us all each other. Dear God, thank you for giving us not only life, but the ability to know that we *are alive*. May we never spend any moment of these hours together ungrateful for the — (*She hesitates.*) — for the splendors which you have given us — here — in this garden of life. (*Pause for a moment; she looks around.*) Now, let's have lunch.

LEMON. (*To the audience.*) My father had romantic feelings about the English countryside. But the spot he chose for our house, not too far from London, was, I always felt, strangely un-English. Particularly in the summer, it seemed to me like a bit of swamp near the Mississippi which had somehow been transported into the English landscape. The air was sticky and hot, the grass and the weeds were as sharp as knives, and as far as the eye could see, a thick scum of tiny insects formed a sort of solid haze between us and the sun. You could hear their noise even inside the house, and when you went outside they were like a storm of tiny pebbles striking your face. All the same, we had a small garden, and when I was five or six or seven or eight, I remember that Aunt Dan and my parents would spend long, long evenings talking in the garden, and I would sit in the grass and listen. (*The garden. Night.*) They used to agree about everything then. (*Mother, Father, and Aunt Dan are laughing. Lemon is apart.*)

FATHER. Did you read that review?

MOTHER. Well, isn't it just the sort of book that Williams would love? He doesn't know a thing about those people himself, but he assumes Antonescu has got it all right.

AUNT DAN. And when Antonescu reads the review, he'll say to himself, "Well then I *did* get it right!" (*They all laugh.*)

LEMON. And they used to play these hilarious games. (*The garden. Night. Mother, Father, and Aunt Dan are playing a game. Aunt Dan is slowly circling around, imitating some animal, and meanwhile tearing some strips of paper. Mother and Father also hold sheets of paper. Lemon is apart, watching.*)

MOTHER. A cat!

FATHER. No, it's sort of a *sea* monster — isn't that it?

MOTHER. A sea *lion*!

FATHER. No — a lion! A lion! (*He rips up pieces of paper.*)

AUNT DAN. Right! A lion!

FATHER. Lion! Lion! (*Mother crumples her sheets of paper and throws them at Father and Aunt Dan. They are all laughing.*)

LEMON. And then there was a time when they stopped playing. And I don't think anyone said, "We shouldn't do this again.

We don't enjoy it any more." I think that even a year later or two years later if you'd asked one of them about it they would have said without any hesitation, "Oh yes, we *love* those games. We play them all the time." (*Pause.*) And then there were wonderful evenings when Aunt Dan and my father and I would listen to my mother reading out loud. (*The garden. Night. Mother is reading out loud inaudibly. Listening are Father, Lemon and Aunt Dan. Lemon speaks to the audience over the reading.*) The sound of her voice was so beautiful. It was so soothing. It made everyone feel calm and at peace. (*As Lemon pauses, the reading becomes audible.*)
MOTHER. Across the dark field the shepherd strode,
His pipe gripped tightly in his gnarled hand,
Heedless of the savage winter rain
Which smote the desolate, barren land.
The sheep had gone; he knew that much,
And out across the tangled wood he struck . . .
LEMON. (*As Mother continues reading inaudibly.*) And then there was a time when she stopped reading. I suppose it was like the games, in a way. There was one evening, some evening, which was the very last time she read to us all, but no one remembered that evening or even noticed it. (*Pause.*) Well, across the garden from the main house was a little house which was also ours. My father had built it to use as a study, but it turned out that he never went near it. And so, somehow, over the years, little by little, I found that I was moving all of my things from my own room in the main house across the garden to this little house, till finally I asked to have my bed moved as well, and so the little house became mine. And it was in that little house, whenever Aunt Dan would come to visit our family, that she and I would have our evening talks, and when I look back on my childhood, it was those talks which I remember more than anything else that ever happened to me. And particularly the talks we had the summer I was eleven years old, which was the last time my parents and Aunt Dan were friends, and Aunt Dan stayed with us for the whole summer, and she came to visit me every night. And in a way it was an amazing thing that a person like Aunt Dan would spend all that time talking to an eleven-year-old child who wasn't even that bright, talking about every complicated subject in the world, but listening to Aunt Dan was the best, the happiest, the most important experience I'd ever had.

21

(*Pause.*) Of course, Aunt Dan wasn't really my aunt. She was one of the youngest Americans to ever teach at Oxford—she was just a couple of years older than my parents—and she was my father's best friend, and my mother's too, and she was always at our house, so to me she was an aunt. Aunt Dan. But my mother and father had other friends, and they had their own lives, and they had each other, and they had me. But I had only Aunt Dan. (*Silence.*) The days that summer were awful and hot. I would sit in the garden with Aunt Dan and Mother, squinting up at the sun to see if it had made any progress in its journey toward the earth. Then, eventually, I would wolf down some tea and bread and by six o'clock I'd be in my little house, waiting for Aunt Dan to come and visit. Because Aunt Dan didn't spend her evenings talking in the garden with my parents any more. And as I waited, my mind would already be filling with all the things she'd told me, the people she'd described. (*Pause.*) Usually there'd still be some light in the sky when I would hear her steps coming up to the little house. And then she would very ceremoniously knock on the door. "Come in!" I'd shout. I'd already be in my pajamas and tucked in under the covers. There'd be a moment's pause. And then she'd come in and sit on my bed. (*Night. The little house. Lemon and Aunt Dan are laughing.*)

AUNT DAN. (*To Lemon.*) You see, the thing was, Geoffrey was the most fantastic liar—I mean, he was so astonishingly handsome, with those gorgeous eyes and those thick, black eyebrows—he just had to look at a woman, with those eyes of his, and she immediately believed every word that he said. And he didn't mind lying to his wife at all, because she'd trapped him into the marriage in the first place, in the most disgusting way, and she just lived off his money, you know—she just lay in bed all day long in a pink housecoat, talking on the telephone and reading magazines and ordering the servants around like slaves. But he knew she'd go mad if he left for the week, so he went to her looking totally tragic, and he said, "Sadie, I've *got* to go to Paris for a conference for at least three days, and I'm so upset, I just hate to leave you, but some professors over there are attacking my theories, and if I don't defend myself my entire reputation will be just destroyed." So she cried and wailed—she was just like a baby—and he promised to bring her lots of pres-

22

ents—and the next thing was, I heard a little knock on my tiny door, and in came Geoffrey into my basement room. I mean, you can't imagine—this tiny room with nothing in it except all my laundry hanging out to dry—and here was this gigantic prince, the most famous professor in the whole university, a great philosopher, coming to see me, a starving second-year student who was living on a diet of brown bread and fruit and occasionally cheese. Well, for the first two days we didn't *move* from bed—I mean, we occasionally reached across to the table and grabbed a pear or an apple or something—and then on the third day we called a taxi, and we went all the way into London to this extraordinary shop—I'd never seen anything like it in my life—and while the taxi waited we simply filled basket after basket with all this incredible food—I mean, outrageous things like hams from Virginia and asparagus from Brussels and paté from France and olives and caviar and boxes of marrons glacés, and then we just piled it all into the taxi, along with bottles and bottles of wine and champagne, and back we went to my tiny basement and spent the rest of the week just living like pigs.

LEMON. The light from the window—the purplish light of the dusk—would fall across her face.

AUNT DAN. Now Lemon, I have to tell you something very important about myself. And there aren't many things I'm sure of about myself, but this is something I can honestly say with absolute confidence, and it's something that I think is very important. It is that I *never*—no matter how annoyed or angry I may be—I *never, ever shout at a waiter.* And as a matter of fact, I never shout at a porter or a clerk in a bank or anybody else who is in a weaker position in society than me. Now this is very, very important. I will never even use a *tone of voice* with a person like that which I wouldn't use with you or your father or anyone else. You see, there are a lot of people today who will simply *shout* if they're angry at a waiter, but if they happen to be angry at some powerful person like their boss or a government official, well then they'll *very respectfully disagree.* Now to me that's a terrible thing, a horrible thing. First of all, because I think it's cowardly. But mainly because it shows that these people don't recognize the value and importance of all those different jobs in society! They think a waiter is less *important* than a president. They look down on waiters! They don't admire what they do! They don't even notice whether someone is a good waiter or a bad waiter! They act as if we could sort of all afford to have no respect for waiters now, or secretaries, or maids, or building superintendents, because somehow we've reached a point where we can really just *do without* these people. Well, maybe there's some kind of a fantasy in these people's minds that we're already living in some society of the future in which these incredible robots are going to be doing all the work, and every actual citizen will be some kind of concert pianist or a sculptor or a president or something. But I mean, where are all these robots, actually? Have you ever seen one? Have they even been invented? Maybe they *will* be. But they're not here *now*. The way things are *now*, everybody just can't *be* a president. I mean—I mean, if there's no one around to cook the president's lunch, he's going to have to cook it himself. Do you know what I'm saying? But if no one has put any food in his kitchen, he's going to have to go out and buy it himself. And if no one is waiting in the shop to sell it, he's going to have to go out into the countryside and *grow* it himself, and, you know, that's going to be a full-time job. I mean, he's going to have to resign as president in order to grow that food. It's as simple as that. If every shop clerk or maid or farmer were to quit their job today and try to be a painter or a nuclear physicist, then within about two weeks *everyone* in society, even people who used to *be* painters or nuclear physicists, would be out in the woods foraging for berries and roots. Society would completely break down. Because regular work is not one tiny fraction less necessary today than it ever was. And yet we're in this crazy situation that people have gotten it into their heads that regular work is somehow unimportant—it's somehow worth nothing. So now almost everyone who isn't at *least* a Minister Of Foreign Affairs feels that there's something wrong with what they do—they feel ashamed of it. Not only do they feel that what they do has no value—they feel actually *humiliated* to be doing it, as if each one of them had been singled out for some kind of unfair, degrading punishment. Each one feels, I shouldn't be a laborer, I shouldn't be a clerk, I shouldn't be a minor official! I'm better than that! And the next thing is, they're saying, "Well, I'll show them all—I won't work, I'll do nothing, or I'll do *almost* nothing, and I'll do it badly." So what's going to happen? We're going to start seeing these embittered typists typing up their documents incorrectly — and then passing them on to these embittered contractors, who will misinterpret them to these huge armies of embittered carpenters and embittered mechanics, and a year later or two years later, we're going to start seeing these ten-story buildings in every city collapsing to the ground, because each one of them is missing some crucial screw in some crucial girder. Buildings will collapse. Planes will come crashing out of the sky. Babies will be poisoned by bad baby food. How can it happen any other way?

LEMON. I would watch the wind gently playing with her hair.

AUNT DAN. Well, that same theater showed vampire films all night long on Saturday nights, and of course all the students would bring these huge bottles of wine into the theater with them, and by the time we got out at dawn on Sunday, your parents and I would be absolutely *mad*. We'd sort of crawl out — dripping with blood — and we'd walk through that freezing town, with everyone asleep, to your father's rooms, and then we'd just close the door and put on some record like Arnold Schoenberg's *Transfigured Night*, as loud as we could. I mean, Lemon, you know, that *Transfigured Night* could just make you squeal, it's just as if Arnold Schoenberg was inside your dress and running his hands over your entire body. And then when we'd drunk about twenty cups of coffee we'd all bicycle out to see some other friends of ours called Phyllis and Ned who lived in a kind of abandoned monastery way out of town, and we would sit outside, and Ned would read us these weird items from the week's papers — you know, he collected horrible stories like "Mother Eats Infant's Head While Father Laughs" and things like that — and Phyllis would serve these gigantic salads out on the grass.

LEMON. And then, as we were talking, night would fall.

AUNT DAN. Well, the telephone thing we worked out was great. Alexander could call me right from his office at the laboratory, no matter who was there, or even from a cozy Sunday afternoon by the fire with his wife, and he'd just say something like, "I need to speak with Dr. Cunningham, please," and that would mean we would meet at Conrad's, a place we used to go to, and then he'd say, "Oh hi, Nat," and that would mean we would meet at nine. Or of course, if I called *him* and his wife answered, I'd just say something like, "I'm awfully sorry, Mrs.

Waldheim, it's Dr. Vetzler's office again," and then he'd get on, and I'd say whatever I had to say, and then he'd say something jaunty like, "Oh hi, Bob! No, that's all right, I don't mind a bit!"

LEMON. But her friends were the best. The people she'd known when she was young and wild and living in London. Amazing people. I felt I knew those people myself. (*Andy appears next to Lemon.*)

ANDY. (*To Lemon.*) Do you remember Mindy? Do you remember June? Do you remember the night that Mindy introduced us to *Jasper*?

LEMON. There was nothing Aunt Dan didn't tell me about them.

ANDY. (*To Lemon.*) Well, June was nice. How could anyone not like June? She was always good-tempered. A wonderful girl. Now, Mindy—Mindy was another story. Mindy could really be sort of annoying, but there were some awfully good reasons for liking her too. For one thing, frankly, she was very, very funny when we were having sex, and that's not nothing. I mean, you know, she thought the whole thing was basically a joke. She just thought bodies were funny, and their little parts were funny, and what they did together was ridiculous and funny. There was just no pressure to make it all work with Mindy, because she really didn't care whether it worked or not. Well, that might be because she used to spend half her day in bed just playing with herself, and she was going out with about six other men as well as me at the time, but from my point of view, I didn't care *why* she was so relaxed about it all, it was just a pleasure, because that was the time when everyone was madly serious about sex, and it was like some kind of terrible hell we all had to go through at the end of each day before we were allowed to go to sleep. And Mindy was different. Mindy thought it was all funny. And you know something else? I really enjoyed giving money to Mindy, because she didn't have it, and she really wanted it, and she loved to get it.

LEMON. Usually Aunt Dan didn't care about politics. In fact, I remember her saying, "When it comes to politics, I'm an ignoramus." But there were certain people Aunt Dan really loved, and one of them was the diplomat Henry Kissinger, who was working for the American government at the time I was eleven. And it reached a kind of point that she was obsessed with Kissinger. When people would criticize him, she would really become extremely upset. Well, this was the time the Americans were fighting in Vietnam, and people even used to attack Kissinger because while all sorts of awful things were happening over there in the war, he was leading the life of a sort of cheerful bachelor in Washington and Hollywood and going out with lots of different girls. People used to say he was an arrogant person. But Aunt Dan defended him.

AUNT DAN. You see, I don't *care* if he's vain or boastful — maybe he is! I don't *care* if he goes out with beautiful girls or likes to ride around on a yacht with millionaires and sheikhs. All right — he enjoys life! Is that a bad thing? If he enjoys life, maybe he'll be even more inspired to do his job of *preserving* life, to help us all lead the life we want! I mean, you can hardly call him a frivolous man. Look at his face! Look at that face! He can stay up night after night after night having a wonderful time with beautiful girls, but he will always have that look on his face, my Lemon, that look of *melancholy* — that look that can't be erased, because he has seen the power of evil in the world.

LEMON. But despite the pain it often caused her, it seemed to me that Aunt Dan just couldn't resist combing every newspaper and every magazine, English and American, to see what they were saying about Kissinger every day.

AUNT DAN. I mean, all right now, Lemon, you know, let's face it — we all know there are countries in this world that are not ideal. They're poor. They're imperfect. Their governments are corrupt. Their water is polluted. But the people in some of these countries are very happy — they have their own farms, they have their own shops, their own political parties, their own newspapers, their own lives that they're leading quietly day by day. And in a lot of these countries the leaders have always been friendly to us, and we've been friendly to them and helped them and supported them. But then what often happens is that there are always some young intellectuals in all of these countries, and they've studied economics at the Sorbonne or Berkeley, and they come home, and they decide to become rebels, and they take up arms, and they eventually throw out the leaders who were friendly to us, and they take over the whole country. Well, pretty soon they start closing the newspapers, and they confiscate the farms, and they set up big camps way out in the country. And people start disappearing. People start getting shot. Well now, this is exactly the kind of situation that Kissinger faces every day. What should he do? Should he give some support to our old friends who are trying to fight these young rebels? Or should he just accept the situation and let the young rebels do what they like? Well Lemon, do you know—it's as if these journalists don't care *what* he does, so long as they can think of a way to put it in some horrible light! I mean, does he decide to let the rebels do what they like? Well then, everyone will say, "This is very unpleasant! All our old friends are being rounded up and slaughtered! Why didn't Kissinger do something to protect these people? They were counting on us, and we betrayed them!" But does he decide instead to help our old friends and fight the young rebels? Well then, he's a bully! He's a thug! He's a warped, raging, vengeful pig who's trying to show off his masculinity by staging a battle with these pitiful, weak, tiny rebels! You know, it's the hypocrisy of it all that makes me want to just crawl to the toilet and vomit, Lemon. I can't believe people can sink so low!

LEMON. And she loved to explain Kissinger's strategies to me.

AUNT DAN. He's trying to get the North Vietnamese in a corner, so they'll have to negotiate on *his terms*. I mean, these North Vietnamese don't care how long this war goes on! *They* don't care how many men they lose! But *we care*. So let's make it worth their while to stop it now! That's why he's being so friendly to the *Chinese* all of a sudden—it's not because he likes Chinese food! Those Chinese are scared of the Russians, so let's help them out—let's give them the feeling they can *relax* a little. Yes, we'll save you from the Russians! Sure! We're glad to! But for God's sake, stop annoying us by being so helpful to those crazy, maniacal North Vietnamese. Please cut it out! And, of course, the Chinese are thrilled to cooperate. It's a small price to pay for an important friendship with us. And so now *we're* in a position to turn around and say to the Russians, "Listen Russians, these damned Chinese are being awfully friendly to us, and we really don't like them, but while this goddamned war in Vietnam is going on, you know, what can we do? We'd much rather be friends with you, but, let's face facts, the way you're supplying these North Vietnamese with guns and tanks, you're actually helping to kill our soldiers every single day, so how can you be shocked if we have some talks with the Chinese — at least they're helping us to end this war!" And the result of all these talks with the Russians and the Chinese is simply going to be that the North Vietnamese are going to be cut off, they're going to be isolated, they're going to *starve.* No supplies from the Chinese! No supplies from the Russians! Pretty soon they're going to understand that. And if they don't understand it, and they keep on acting as if they can do what they like, well, all the better. We'll bomb their harbors, we'll bomb their cities, and then we'll sit and watch while the Russians and Chinese make a few little critical noises and proceed to do absolutely *nothing* to help them. And when the North Vietnamese feel *that* knife in the heart from their supposed allies, then they'll finally, finally understand that they have *no options.*

LEMON. And there was a story she told me more than once.

AUNT DAN. It was utterly amazing. I could hardly believe it, my little Lemon. It was last winter, and I had a date to have lunch one day at this club in Washington. Well, as I entered the rather formal room where one waited for one's luncheon partner in this rather disgusting, rather unbearable club — and I was waiting to meet a rather disgusting, rather unbearable friend, a member of the club — I saw, sitting in an armchair, reading a large manuscript, Henry Kissinger. At first I couldn't believe it was really Kissinger — why in the world would he be there in this terrible place? But, of course, it *was* him, and he undoubtedly had come for the very same reason that I had — a sense of loyalty, a sense of obligation, to some old but now perhaps rather stupid friend. And it was possible that Kissinger was early, but it was also possible that that friend of Kissinger's was indeed *so* stupid that he actually was late to his own lunch with Henry Kissinger. Of course I tried not to stare. I took a seat far across the room. But every now and then I would just peep over and look. And the most striking thing was that, seated in an uncomfortable position in this uncomfortable chair, Kissinger was utterly immobile. Each time I looked over, his position was exactly the same as it had been before. His pose was more or less determined by what he was doing — he was reading the manuscript held in his lap — but to me the downward-looking angle of his entire head, so characteristic of Kissinger, expressed something more — my feeling was that it expressed the habitual humility of a man whose attitude to life was, actually, prayerful, a man, I felt, who was living in fear of an all-knowing God. The boastful exuberance of the public Kissinger was nowhere to be seen in this private moment. Kissinger's thoughts were not on himself, they were on what was written in that large manuscript — and from that same downward look you could tell that the manuscript was not some theoretical essay, not some analysis of something that had happened a hundred years ago, but a document describing some crucial problem which had to be dealt with by Kissinger soon; and in Kissinger's heart I felt I could see one and only one question nervously beating — would he make the right decision about that problem? Would he have the wisdom to do the thing that would help to resolve it, or would he be misled, would he make an error in judgment and act, somehow, so as to make things worse? Let me tell you, there was no arrogance in the man who sat in that uncomfortable, ridiculous armchair, waiting for his stupid friend to come to lunch; that was a man saddened, almost *terrified*, by the awful thought that he might just possibly do something wrong, that he might just possibly make some dreadful mistake. Then, suddenly, Kissinger's friend arrived — stupid, just as I'd predicted, but so much *more* stupid than I would ever have imagined — a huge, vulgar, crew-cutted, red-faced, overgrown baby who greeted Kissinger with a twanging voice and pumped his hand about twenty times. But, my God, the warmth with which Kissinger leapt up and greeted this man! It was almost impossible to believe. I was utterly stunned by the sheer *joy* which turned Kissinger's face as red as his friend's and seemed to banish from his mind all thought of the heavy manuscript which he still clutched mechanically in his left hand. But then, yes, I realized — this is a man who loves his country, and he loves the people of his country. To Kissinger, I felt, the very crudeness and grossness of this man were his most American, and therefore almost his most wonderful, features, and that was why Kissinger now was smiling like Punch himself in a puppet show as he chatted and laughed with this ignorant, brutal, piglike American friend. And then off they went to the dining room, and I stayed behind and waited for my own stupid friend, and he got from me a greeting that was much less generous, much less kind. But am I proud of myself, Lemon, for my chilly, indifferent greeting toward my stupid friend? No, I'm not. And do I admire Kissinger for his ardent love of a country and a people that have offered him, and perhaps could still offer the entire world, the hope of a safe and decent future? Yes. Yes. I admire him for that.

LEMON. Naturally, at that time, I often used to dream about running away from my parents and going to live with Aunt Dan in London, and I must admit I often pictured that Kissinger would be dropping in on us fairly regularly there. At least, I imagined, he would never think of missing Sunday breakfast, Aunt Dan's favorite meal. For Kissinger, I imagined, she'd always prepare something very special, like some little tarts, or eggs done up with brandy and cream. And Kissinger, I felt, would be at his very most relaxed around Aunt Dan. He would stretch himself out on the big couch with a sleepy sort of smile on his face, and he and Aunt Dan would gossip like teenagers, both of them saying outrageous things and trying their best to shock each other. As for myself, the truth was that I was quite prepared to serve Kissinger as his personal slave—I imagined he liked young girls as slaves. Well, he could have his pleasure with me, I'd decided long ago, if the occasion ever arose. Few formalities would need to be observed—he didn't have the time, and I knew that very well. An exchange of looks, then right to bed—that would be fine with me. It wasn't how I planned to live as a general rule, but for Kissinger, I thought, I would make an exception. He served humanity. I would serve him. (*Pause.*) But a lot of people didn't feel about Kissinger the way we did, and after a while we realized something that we both found rather surprising. As it turned out, one of the people who didn't like Kissinger was actually Mother! In fact, Mother didn't like him even at all—just not one bit—and throughout that summer, when Mother and Aunt Dan would chat in the garden in the afternoons, whenever the conversation turned to the subject of Kissinger, as it often did—and more and *more* often, it seemed to me—things would suddenly become extremely tense. And, naturally, at the time I wasn't in a position to see these conversations as steps toward a final split between Mother and Aunt Dan, but that, of course, was exactly what they were. (*The garden. A silence before Aunt Dan speaks.*)

AUNT DAN. Susie, do you think he *likes* to bomb a village full of poor peasants?

MOTHER. (*After a long pause.*) Dan, if you're asking whether I think he personally enjoys it—I have no idea. I don't know. I don't know him.

AUNT DAN. Susie! My God! What a horrible thing to say!

MOTHER. Well Dan, after all, there *are* people who for one reason or another . . . just can't control their lust for blood, or they just give in totally to that side of their nature. They convince themselves that it's necessary—

AUNT DAN. You think that *Kissinger*—

MOTHER. No, Dan, I don't know him, really. I have no idea. (*Pause.*) I'm sure he believes that what he's doing is right—that he can't avoid it—

AUNT DAN. Mmm-hmm—

MOTHER. But you know, he could believe that he had to do it—he could feel that he was only striking out against a danger, an immediate, terrible danger, a threat, to America—or the world—but you know still it could be . . . a delusion, actually. I mean, what if the threat is a fantasy, Dan, or what if it isn't really—so utterly crucial?

AUNT DAN. But Susie, he assesses that. That's exactly what he does all day.

MOTHER. No, I'm sure he does, but sometimes people don't assess things carefully enough, because they've really already made up their minds about them a long time ago. They think they're studying all the information, but actually their preconceptions are so strong that they're not really paying very close attention—do you know what I mean? (*Aunt Dan is silent.*)

LEMON. And so the hot afternoons in the garden got worse and worse, and the cool, blessed evenings in the little house, where Aunt Dan would tell me about her friends, by contrast, seemed nicer and nicer. And the amazing thing is that still, in my memory, the afternoons and evenings of that long summer keep following each other, on and on, in an endless alternation. (*Mindy appears next to Lemon.*) And as the early days of August grew into the late days, Aunt Dan told me more and more about her friend Mindy.

MINDY. (*To Lemon.*) I was living a sort of dog's life at that time, quite frankly. I always seemed to be making furious love on top of ugly bedspreads and then taking these awful showers

32

with strange men. But Andy was always so sweet to me.

AUNT DAN. (*To Mother.*) Susie, look, he has to make a choice. He has to fight or not fight. One or the other. Do you want him not to fight? Fine — then any country in the world will be free from now on to do anything they like, and we'll be free to do nothing. If they want to invade other countries, or conquer other people's territory, or kill all our friends, well then that's all okay, that's all fine. But some day somebody is going to lose their patience. Do you see what I'm saying? And then you just might find yourself falling into a war that is suddenly so big that you can't stop it.

MOTHER. I understand, you *think* that if America doesn't fight in Vietnam today, then more and more countries in the world will come to be America's enemies. In ten years. In twenty years. But that's just a prediction. It's just a guess.

AUNT DAN. Yes. It's a prediction.

MINDY. (*To Lemon.*) And it would be late at night, and I'd be sitting in some quiet flat with the clock ticking gently, and I'd be looking at some man whom I'd caressed and hugged, and whose beautifully wrapped presents I'd opened in a gay flurry of shrieks and cries — jewelry, perfume, or lingerie — and he'd be dressed in some endearing underwear, and he'd be telling me quietly about the secrets of his life, and suddenly something would come over me, and a cold sweat would break out on my face, and the most incredible lies, or strange insults, would come out of my mouth, and I would rush to the door and go out into the street. And it was a wonderful thing, on a night like that, to find a telephone and call Andy. And he would always tell me to come right over. And it was really nice on those particular nights to just stick my hand in the air and hail a taxi and go over and play with Andy and his friends.

AUNT DAN. (*To Mother.*) Susie, he is not a private individual like you and me — he works for the *government*! I mean, you're talking here as if you were trying to tell me that you and I are so nice every day and why can't our governments be just like us! I can't believe you're saying that! Don't you understand that you and I are only able to be nice because our governments — our governments are *not* nice? Why do you think we've set these things up? I mean, a state, policemen, politicians — what's it all for? The point is so we don't all have to spend our lives in some

33

ditch by the side of the road fighting like animals about every little thing. The whole purpose of government is to use force. So we don't have to. So if I move into your house and refuse to leave, you don't have to kick me or punch me, you don't have to go find some acid to throw in my face — you just nicely have to pick up the phone and call the police! And if some other country attacks our friends in Southeast Asia, you and I don't have to go over there and fight them with rifles — we just get Kissinger to fight them for us.

MOTHER. But Dan —

AUNT DAN. These *other* people use force, so we can sit here in this garden and be incredibly nice. Otherwise we'd be going around covered with scars and bruises and our hair all torn out, like stray cats.

MOTHER. But are you saying that governments can do anything, or Kissinger can do anything, and somehow it's never proper for us to say, Well we don't like this, we think this is wrong? Do you mean to say that we don't have the right to criticize this person's decisions? That no one has the right to criticize them?

AUNT DAN. No, I don't say that. Go right ahead. Criticize his decisions all you like. I don't know. Go ahead and criticize everything he does.

MOTHER. I don't —

AUNT DAN. Particularly if you have no idea what you would do in his place.

MOTHER. Dan, I'm not . . . (*Silence.*)

AUNT DAN. Susie, I'm simply saying that it's terribly easy for us to criticize. It's terribly easy for us to sit here and give our opinions on the day's events. And while we sit here in the sunshine and have our discussions about what we've read in the morning papers, there are these certain *other* people, like Kissinger, who happen to have the very bad luck to be society's leaders. And while we sit here chatting, they have to do what has to be done. And so *we* chat, but *they* do what they *have* to do. *They* do what they *have* to do. And if they have to do something, they're prepared to do it. Because I'm very sorry, if you're in a position of responsibility, that means you're responsible for doing whatever it is that has to be done. If you're on the outside, you can wail and complain about what society's leaders are doing. Go ahead. That's fine. That's your right. That's your privileged position. But if you are the one who's in power, if you're responsible, if you're a leader, you don't have that privilege. It's your job to do it. Just to do it. Do it. Do it. Don't complain, don't agonize, don't moan, don't wail. Just do it. Everyone will hate you. Fine. That's their right. But you have to do it. Of course, you're defending *those very people. They're* the ones you're defending. But do you expect to be *understood?* You must be nuts! You must be crazy! — insane! All day long you're defending *them* — defending, defending, defending — and your reward is, they'll spit in your face! All right — so be it. That's the way it is. The joy of leadership. But you can bet that what Kissinger says when he goes to bed at night is, Dear God, I wish I were nothing. Dear God, I wish I were a little child. I wish I were a bird or a fish or a deer living quietly in the woods. I wish I were anything but what I am. I am a slave, but they see me as a master. I am sacrificing my life for them, but they think I'm scrambling for power for myself. For myself! Myself! *None* of it is for myself. I *have* no self. I am a leader — that means I am a slave, I am less than dirt. *They* think of themselves. *I* don't. They think, what would *I* like? What would be nice for *me?* I think, what has to be done? What is the thing I *must* do? I don't think, what would be nice for *me* to do? No. No. Never. Never. Never that. Only, what is the thing I *must* do? What is the thing I *must* do. (*Silence.*) And then these filthy, slimy worms, the little journalists, come along, and it is so far beyond their comprehension — and in a way it's so unacceptable to them — that anyone could possibly be motivated by dreams that are loftier than their own pitiful hopes for a bigger byline, or a bigger car, or a girlfriend with a bigger bust, or a house with a bigger game-room in the basement, that, far from feeling gratitude to this man who has taken the responsibility for making the most horrible, shattering decisions, they feel they can't rest till they make it impossible for him to continue! They're out to stop him! Defying the father figure, the big daddy! Worms! Worms! How *dare* they attack him for killing peasants? What decisions did *they* make today? What did *they* have to decide, the little journalists? What did *they* have to decide? Did they decide whether to write one very long column or two tiny little columns? Did they decide whether to have dinner at their favorite French restaurant or to save a little money by going to their second-favorite French restaurant instead? Cowards! Cowards! If anyone brought them a decision that involved human life, where people would die whatever they decided, they would run just as fast as their little legs would carry them. But they're not afraid of trying to stop *him*, of making people have contempt for *him*, of stirring up a storm of loathing for *him*, of keeping him so busy fending off their attacks that he can't breathe, he can't escape, he just has to collapse or resign! I would love to see these cowards face up to some of the consequences of their murder of our leaders! I would love to see them face some of the little experiences our leaderless soldiers face when they suddenly meet the North Vietnamese in the middle of the jungle. That might make the little journalists understand what they were doing, the little cowards. Have they ever felt a bayonet go right through their chest? Have they ever felt a knife rip right through their guts? Would they be sneering then, would they be thinking up clever ways to mock our leaders? No, they'd be squealing like pigs, they'd be begging, begging, "Please save me! Please help me!" I would love to be hiding behind a tree watching the little cowards screaming and bleeding and shitting in their pants! I would love to be watching! Those slimy cowards. So let's see them try to make some decisions. Let's see them decide that people have to die. They wouldn't have the faintest idea what to do. But they just sit in their offices and write their little columns. They just sit in their offices and toss them off. Well, do you think Kissinger is just sitting in *his* office casually making his *decisions*? Do you think he makes those decisions lightly? What do you think? Do you think he just sits in his office and tosses them off? Do you think he just makes them in two minutes between bites of a sandwich? (*A long silence.*)

MOTHER. Dan, I'm sure he makes his decisions thoughtfully. And I'm sure he believes himself to be justified. But I was asking, is he *actually* justified, as far as *I* am concerned? I'm sure he's weighed those lives in the balance against . . . some large objective. But I was asking, has he weighed them, actually, at — at what I would consider their correct measure? (*A silence.*) Does he have a heart which is capable of weighing them correctly?

AUNT DAN. What? What? I don't believe this! I don't believe

what I'm hearing from you! Look, I'm sorry, Susie, but all I can say to you is that if he sat at his desk weeping and sobbing all day, I don't think he'd be able to do his job. That's all I can say. He has just as much of a heart as anyone else, you can be sure of that, but the point is that the heart by itself cannot tell you what to do in a situation like that. The heart just responds to the present moment — it just sees these people in a village who've been hit by a bomb, and they're wounded and dying, and it's terribly sad. But the mind — the mind sees the story through to the end. It sees that yes, there are people who are wounded and dying in that village. But if we *hadn't* bombed it, some of those same people would have been marching tomorrow toward the *next* village with the grenades and machine guns they'd stored in that pretty little church we blew up, and when they *got* to that village, they would have burned it to the ground and raped the women and tortured the men and killed whole families — mothers and children. Of course, those things aren't actually happening now, so the heart doesn't care about them. But the things that will happen tomorrow are real too. When it *is* tomorrow, they'll be just as real as the things that are happening now. So I'm asking you, Susie, here is Kissinger. Here is the man who must make the decisions. What do you want this man to do? I am only asking what you want him to do. What is it that you want him to do?

MOTHER. (*After a long pause.*) Well, I suppose I want him to assess the threat he is facing . . . with scrupulous honesty . . . and then I want him to think about those people. Yes, I suppose I do want him to weep and sob at his desk. Yes. Then let him make his decisions.

LEMON. There were times when Aunt Dan just stared at Mother. She just sat and stared. (*Andy appears next to Lemon.*)

ANDY. Well, Mindy would do almost anything, you know, to get hold of money, but with all the good will in the world she still ended up at times without a penny in her purse. And it was at times like that that the phone would ring in the middle of the night, and there would be Mindy asking what I was up to. Well, I was usually flat on my back being fucked by some girl, if you'll pardon my French, or maybe two, but that didn't bother Mindy a bit. She'd come by for some money, and half the time she'd stay to have sex with the rest of us as well. The one thing the girls I liked seemed to have in common was they all liked Mindy—but I mean, who wouldn't? She was so thin she never took up any room, and she never asked anyone for anything but money. In my book, she was okay. Well, you see, they say the English are stuffy, but that's not my experience. (*Andy's flat. Late night. Mindy and Jasper are coming in the door, amidst hilarity. Andy, June, and Aunt Dan—in her early thirties—are hastily putting on dressing-gowns or long sweaters.*)

ANDY. Well, well, well—hello, Mindy. What's this?

MINDY. Hello, Andy. I've brought you Jasper. (*Presenting him with a grand gesture. Whoops from everyone. Andy makes introductions.*)

ANDY. Delighted, Jasper. June and Dan. (*Everyone mock-formally shakes hands, murmuring loudly.*)

MINDY. (*To Andy.*): You see, Jasper's new in town, passing through, a countryman of yours.

ANDY. What, mine?

MINDY. Say hello, Jasper. Show Andy you're one of his.

ANDY. Now don't be rude, Mindy—he may be shy! Don't make him talk like a puppet. I think he *is* shy. Let him take his time. Shall we have some drinks? June, help me, dear, ask Jasper what he'd like—what about you, Mindy?

MINDY. Vodka, please.

ANDY. A beer for me—

AUNT DAN. Bourbon for me.

JASPER. Oh, can I help? (*June and Jasper exit.*)

ANDY. So who's this Jasper?

MINDY. Well I just met him. He's got a hundred thousand pounds in his trouser pocket.

ANDY. What? Really?

MINDY. He won it. Gambling.

AUNT DAN. My my.

ANDY. Yes, good for you. I hope you get twenty off him at least.

MINDY. Jesus Christ, I'd really like it all.

ANDY. Well, not *all*. That's not fair, Mindy. Leave him a little.

MINDY. If the poor guy would just have a heart attack and die on your floor, we could keep every penny and no one would know. I mean, he's here as a tourist, all by himself. We met in the park. He's been wandering around since he won the money.

38

He's lived a good life! And he's a worthless person, I promise you no one would miss him. He's already told me, his wife hates his guts.

ANDY. Why don't you tell him you need the money?

MINDY. I tried that—it didn't work. (*Jasper and June return.*)

JUNE. Jasper's telling me the most amazing story. I think he's frightfully clever.

JASPER. Look, Andy, I won a hundred thousand pounds tonight, from about six guys in a gambling casino. I don't know how it happened, unless they rigged the deck, and somehow it worked out wrong—I mean, they made some mistake and instead of them getting the cards it turned out to be me. I mean, I just kept winning—I'd win one hand, and then I'd win again, and then I'd win again, and each time the stakes kept getting bigger—I think they must have thought that each time it would go against me, but it never did. God damn—my mother would have loved to hear this story—she never saw money in her whole life.

JUNE. God damn—neither did *my* mother, come to think of it.

MINDY. Mine neither.

ANDY. Well, since you ask, *my* mother is quite all right. And how about yours, Dan—is she doing all right?

AUNT DAN. Oh, not too bad.

JASPER. I mean, I'll tell you, Andy, these British men really like to spend money. They're wild as hell.

ANDY. I've found that myself, I must admit.

JUNE. Where have I been all my life?

ANDY. Oh come on, June, now what about that fellow you were telling me about just last week? A Member of Parliament, Jasper, who took June to Africa to study some natives on an important commission about something or other. He used to buy elephants' tusks as if they were pencils—he gave you so many presents you had to hire a little boat to carry them all through the swamps, you told me.

JUNE. Not the swamps, dear, that was the *vaal.*

ANDY. Well pardon me, the *vaal* then.

JUNE. I can't stand how these Yankees can't speak the language.

ANDY. Oh we do all right, we know the major phrases.

JASPER. Yeah, like, "Place your bets," "Let's try another

39

hand"—

ANDY. Yes, right, exactly, things like that—

JUNE. But what part of America do you come from, Jasper?

JASPER. Oh, I'm from Chicago—

AUNT DAN. Aha—

JUNE. Great. I've heard they make the most marvelous steaks. It's just like being a cave man again, a friend of mine said.

JASPER. What do you mean?

ANDY. I think you're thinking of Poughkeepsie, dear.

JUNE. No, that's where they make that white cheese that you put on top of fish.

AUNT DAN. Philadelphia.

JUNE. No, that sounds Greek. Wait—it's a Greek island! Yes, I went there once with a big fisherman. I didn't understand a word he said, but he certainly knew how to catch fish.

AUNT DAN. That's *not* Philadelphia.

ANDY. Well it *might* be, somehow. Is that where you learned how to mend nets? Didn't you once tell me you could mend nets?

JUNE. Who, me?

MINDY. Look, Jasper, you're neglecting that scotch.

JASPER. God you're pretty—you know, I really like you.

MINDY. I told you, Jasper—I have a serious boyfriend, you're not allowed to think of me like that—don't look at me like that, I'm telling you, Jasper, or I'm just going to send you home in a cab.

ANDY. She's serious, Jasper—it's hopeless, my friend, I've tried for years.

JASPER. Years? What? You don't really have a boyfriend, do you, you weasel? I mean, what is this "years"? If it's been all these years, then where's the boyfriend? He's just an excuse. He doesn't exist. Does he, Andy?

ANDY. Well, I must admit, *I've* never met him. But she's sure been faithful to the guy, I'll say that much.

JASPER. But is there really a guy, or are you just a tease?

MINDY. What is this, Jasper, are you calling me a liar?

JASPER. Yes, I am. You know you'll have me if I give you money.

MINDY. Hey, wow—now don't insult me.

JASPER. Well, I'd love to have you without the money, but

40

you told me no. So now I'm asking you *with* the money.

MINDY. Is that what you're saying? And you think I would?

JASPER. For a thousand pounds, no. That would be too cheap—just prostitution. But *ten* thousand pounds, that's more like marriage. That would be like an intensely serious, permanent relationship, except it wouldn't last beyond tomorrow morning.

MINDY. No, Jasper.

JASPER. What is this no? Are you totally nuts?

MINDY. Give me all of it!

JASPER. Get lost!

JUNE. I think this discussion is going in circles.

ANDY. Friends, please! Let's try to approach our problems sensibly, all right? Now, Jasper, you're asking very little of Mindy, in my opinion. You merely want to strip her clothes off for a few hours and probably fuck her twice at the most, and for this you are offering her ten thousand pounds. Mindy, *my* opinion is, the exchange would be worth it. June, don't you think so? Tell us your opinion.

JUNE. Jasper seems to me an attractive man. He's extremely polite, he's extremely friendly. I'd be very surprised if he had any diseases—diseases, Jasper?

JASPER. Absolutely not. Do you think this kind of thing is my normal life? I *never* do this. I'm on vacation. Now here's the situation: I'm going back home tomorrow morning, and I'm going to put this money in the bank, and right now I'd like to spend some—ten thousand pounds.

JUNE. I think it's a good idea.

MINDY. For ten thousand pounds you can see my tits.

ANDY. Please, Mindy, let's not turn my flat into an oriental market. Either go to bed with the nice man or send him home, but please don't sit on my sofa and sell different parts of yourself. Besides, if you start dividing yourself into pieces, how do you know we won't each take a section and end up tearing you to bits?

MINDY. I don't want your money—I want his.

JUNE. I notice she doesn't mention mine. I'll bet she's guessed I don't *have* any. (*A pause.*)

AUNT DAN. I'll throw in five pounds just to watch.

ANDY. Well, I'll pay a hundred pounds *not* to watch, and here it is. (*He puts it on the table and gets up.*) Come on, June.

AUNT DAN. (*To Lemon.*): Well, Mindy was a terribly clever girl, and she managed to get an awful lot of money from poor Jasper. She really did get ten thousand for taking off her shirt, and by the time he'd screwed her she'd got sixty thousand. Meanwhile, he was trying to pay *me* just to leave the room, but I wouldn't budge. Finally he was so drunk and exhausted he fell asleep, and Mindy sat there on that sofa stark naked and told me stories about her life. Outside the window the city was sleeping, but Mindy's eyes sparkled as she talked on and on. There wasn't much that she hadn't done, and there were things she didn't tell anyone about, but she told me. (*Mindy is seen with Freddie, an American man.*)

MINDY. (*To Freddie.*): All right, I'll do it. Sure. Why not. But you're giving me the money now, right?

FREDDIE. Sure. Of course. I'll see you at Morley's tomorrow evening at nine o'clock. We'll work it so when we come in you'll have a date already—it's more fun that way. And we'll call you Rosa.

MINDY. Okay, Freddie. Whatever you like. (*Morley's, a night club. Raimondo, Freddie, and Flora enter. Mindy and Marty are already at a table. Marty is an American man. Flora is a young American woman.*)

MARTY. Hey! Freddie!

FREDDIE. Marty! Rosa! How unexpected!

MARTY. Oh—you know Rosa?

FREDDIE. I've known her for years. A marvelous girl—what's she doing with a guy like you, Marty? (*They all laugh.*) Marty, Rosa, this is Flora Mansfield, and this is my very good friend Raimondo Lopez.

MARTY. Flora. Raimondo.

RAIMONDO. Delighted. Señorita—

MINDY. Enchantée, I'm sure.

MARTY. Say, but where the hell is your wife, Freddie?

FREDDIE. My what? No, no, just kidding, Marty, Corrine's in the country with all the boys—

MARTY. Great. Great. But—er—listen, Freddie, why don't you and your friends join Rosa and me—

FREDDIE. Oh we'd hate to trouble you—

MARTY. No, really—

FREDDIE. Really? Do you think—? Well—er—Raimondo—would you like—?

RAIMONDO. Well yes—yes—certainly—yes. (*Music. They sit down.*)

FLORA. (*To Marty.*) Say—do you have a brother who sells room dividers over on Bamberger Street?

MARTY. Well—no.

FLORA. Gosh—there's a guy over there who looks exactly like you.

FREDDIE. Er—just imagine. (*They all listen to the music for a while.*)

RAIMONDO. (*To Mindy.*) What absolutely wonderful music—really delightful—

MINDY. Yes—isn't it?

RAIMONDO. It reminds me of—er—Brasilia Chantelle—do you know that group?

MINDY. No—

RAIMONDO. They have a vibraphone, a banjo, a sax, and a harp. Not your ordinary combo—eh? (*They laugh.*)

MINDY. You seem to know a lot about music, Mr. Lopez.

RAIMONDO. Well, music is one of my passions, you see—you know, I'm afraid I didn't catch your last name.

MINDY. Er—Gatti.

RAIMONDO. Italian?

MINDY. On my father's side Italian. My mother was English.

RAIMONDO. She's no longer living?

MINDY. Yes—she died last winter. A terrible illness.

RAIMONDO. I'm very sorry.

MINDY. Oh, thank you, really. Do you like this wine?

RAIMONDO. It's delicious. It's special.

MINDY. Yes, it's Italian.—The sparkling wines of that region are always—

RAIMONDO. You picked it?

MINDY. Yes.

RAIMONDO. You like wine, don't you?

MINDY. Not *too* much, no—

RAIMONDO. I didn't say *too* much—

MINDY. You were thinking it, though—You were thinking I look like the kind of person—

RAIMONDO. *Every* person is that kind of person. I'm a student of the subject. Ha ha! Believe me. But I like it, too. When a wine is good—and the company's amusing—

MINDY. When the company's amusing, *any* wine is good. (*They laugh.*)

RAIMONDO. You're single, then, Miss Gatti? That's almost Italian for cat, isn't it? It's the same word in Spanish—

MINDY. Yes. Yes. I'm single. Miss Cat, if you like.

RAIMONDO. Yes—yes—I'll call you Miss Cat. (*They laugh.*) And when you put that fur around your neck, I'll bet that you look like one too, Miss Cat.

MINDY. Oh come on.

RAIMONDO. No, I mean it. Your smile is a little bit cat-like too.

MINDY. You've just got the idea in your head, Mr. Lopez.

RAIMONDO. What idea? Now what idea do I have in my head? (*They are both laughing.*) Are you telling me what ideas I have in my head now? (*They both laugh loudly.*) You're a very unusual woman, Gatti. I think you can *put* ideas inside people's heads if you really want to.

MINDY. Say—now what in the world are you talking about? Eh?

RAIMONDO. If you only *knew* the ideas you've put in my head.

MINDY. I think you're crazy! That's what I think, Mr. Lopez—I think you're absolutely mad!

RAIMONDO. I think you're a witch! I think you're a devil!

MINDY. (*A roar of laughter from the other side of the table.*) Say—it looks like Marty is flirting with your date!

RAIMONDO. My date? Are you crazy? That's not my date! That's a friend of Freddie's wife, a very close friend of his family, Gatti!

MINDY. Oh she is, eh?

RAIMONDO. Yes!—she is! A friend of his family!

MINDY. Really!

RAIMONDO. Yes!

MINDY. Well, all right, Mr. Lopez, then I think Marty is flirting with a very close friend of Freddie's family. (*Outside of Morley's. The same group.*)

MARTY. Well, Rosa, let me take you home. Ha ha—we've hardly had a chance to talk all evening! Now—you live on the

South Side, don't you, Rosa?

FREDDIE. Well, why don't we all share a cab? Flora lives on the South Side too—

FLORA. Yes—good—

MARTY. That's fine—great—

MINDY. Well, Freddie, actually, I live on the North Side, actually—

MARTY. Oh—well—

RAIMONDO. So Marty—why don't you drop Freddie and Flora, and *I'll* take Rosa along with me—

MARTY. Oh well, really—oh no—(*to Mindy*) are you sure you wouldn't mind?

MINDY. No no—not at all—

MARTY. Well then—er—all right—well then, come along, Flora—you come along with us—

FLORA. Oh I see—all right—

RAIMONDO. (*To Mindy.*) And you come with me. (*Mindy's apartment. Raimondo and Mindy are standing at different sides of the room. They have come in a few minutes before. A silence.*) Do you know the first glimpse I had of you tonight?

MINDY. No—what was it?

RAIMONDO. I was standing in the entrance to the restaurant, and Flora was checking her coat, and I looked into the room, and I mostly saw these men in their boring jackets and ties and these dull-looking women—and just through a crack between all those people I suddenly saw a pair of lavender stockings, and I wondered, who is the person who belongs to those stockings? (*They both laugh.*) Because I'm a connoisseur of women's clothing, Gatti. From a woman's clothing, you can see everything. Because some clothing is inert and dead, just dead cloth, like dead skins. And some clothing is alive. Some clothing is there just to cover the body. And some is there to—to describe the body, to tell you about it—like a beautiful wrapping on something sweet. (*There is a silence. He walks toward her. Then he crouches on the floor in front of her and slides his hands along her stockings. He puts his head up her skirt.*) Oh—so warm. (*She stays absolutely still, neither encouraging nor resisting. After a moment, he removes his head and looks at her. Then he helps her take off her shoes, and he removes her stockings. He puts them over the back of a chair.*)

MINDY. Would you like a drink?

RAIMONDO. Well—would you?

MINDY. Thank you. Yes. There's some brandy—there—(*She points to the brandy. He gets up, gets them both a drink. He sips his.*)

MINDY. Won't you take off that jacket?

RAIMONDO. Oh—thank you—yes. (*He takes off his jacket and tie.*)

MINDY. Sit down, why don't you. (*He sits. There is a silence.*)

RAIMONDO. You're so gorgeous—so sweet. You know, when I get hungry, I'm just like a bear. I start to sweat till I get to the honey.

MINDY. Finish your brandy. There's plenty of time. (*She wipes his forehead with a napkin as he sips his drink. As he finishes, she lowers herself to the floor in front of him, unzips his trousers and starts to kiss his crotch.*)

RAIMONDO. Oh God—yes—yes—oh, please—(*After another moment, she looks up.*)

MINDY. It's chilly in here. And you're still sweating. Come lie down. (*Raimondo starts to stand.*)

RAIMONDO. I feel dizzy.

MINDY. Just relax. (*They head toward the bedroom. She turns back for her stockings.*)

RAIMONDO. I feel dizzy. (*In the darkness, his cries of ecstasy.*) Oh, beautiful. Oh, good. (*The bedroom. The light from the window falls on the stockings. Mindy is standing by the bed, dressed in a robe, looking down at Raimondo, who is out cold. She shakes him roughly, and he groans slightly but doesn't wake up. Then she opens a drawer, pulls on a pair of jeans, takes out some pieces of rope, and loops them around the knobs at the head of the bed and the knobs at the foot. She slips the nooses around Raimondo's wrists and ankles. She picks up the pair of stockings, and he suddenly speaks. His voice is indistinct.*) Rosa? Rosa? (*She freezes. After a moment, he feels the ropes, then speaks again, a bit louder.*) What are you doing? Rosa? (*She steps onto the bed behind him.*) Rosa! Please! No! No! (*She puts her feet on his shoulders, leans back against the headboard, puts the stockings around his neck and starts to strangle him. She looks straight ahead of her, not at his face, as he struggles and gags.*)

AUNT DAN. (*To Lemon.*) She had to put the guy in this plastic sack, kick him down her back stairs, haul him outside, and stick him into the trunk of a car that was parked in an alley. Apparently he'd been working with the police for some time against her friend, Freddie. (*A silence.*) Well. My teeth were chattering as I listened to the words of this naked goddess, whose lipstick was the dreamiest, loveliest shade of rose. Then she fell silent for a long time, and we just looked at each other. And then she sort of winked at me, I think you would call it, and I wanted to touch that lipstick with my fingers, so I did. And she sort of grabbed my hand and gave it a big kiss, and my hand was all red. And then we just sat there for another long time. And then, to the music of Jasper snoring on the couch, I started to kiss her beautiful neck. I was incredibly in love. She kissed me back. I felt as if stars were flying through my head. She was gorgeous, perfect. We spent the rest of the night on the couch, and then we went out and had a great breakfast, and we spent a wonderful week together. (*Pause.*)

LEMON. (*To Aunt Dan.*) Why only a week?

AUNT DAN. Huh?

LEMON. Why only a week? (*Pause.*)

AUNT DAN. Lemon, you know, it's because . . . (*Pause.*) Because love always cries out to be somehow expressed. (*Pause.*) But the expression of love leads somehow—nowhere. (*A silence.*) You express love, and suddenly you've . . . you've dropped off the map you were on, in a way, and onto another one—unrelated—like a bug being brushed from the edge of a table and falling off onto the rug below. The beauty of a face makes you touch a hand, and suddenly you're in a world of actions, of experiences, unrelated to the beauty of that face, unrelated to that face at all, unrelated to beauty. You're doing things and saying things you never wanted to say or do. You're suddenly spending every moment of your life in conversations, in encounters, that have no connection with anything you ever wanted for yourself. What you felt was love. What you felt was that the face was beautiful. And it was not enough for you just to feel love, just to sit in the presence of beauty and enjoy it. Something about your feeling itself made that impossible. And so you just didn't ask, Well, what will happen when I touch that hand? What will happen between that person and me? What will even happen to the thing I'm feeling at this very moment? Instead, you just walked right off that table, and there was that person, with all their qualities, and there was you, with all *your*

47

qualities, and there you were together. And it's always, of course, extremely fascinating for as long as you can stand it, but it has nothing to do with the love you originally felt. Every time, in a way, you think it will have *something* to do with the love you felt. But it never does. It never has anything to do with love. (*Silence.*)

LEMON. (*To the audience.*) My father didn't know about my mother's conversations with Aunt Dan in the garden. He had other things on his mind. The friendship ended, it faded away, and it didn't bother him. Aunt Dan never came back to visit us after the summer I was eleven, but a couple of times a year I would take the train into London and visit her, and she would take me out to dinner at some beautiful restaurant, and we'd sit together and have a lovely meal and talk for hours. When I was just eighteen, Aunt Dan got sick, and then when I was nineteen she finally died. (*Pause.*) In the year or two before Aunt Dan got sick there would sometimes be some odd moments, some crazy moments, in those beautiful restaurants. Some moments when both of us would just fall silent. Well, it was really quite straightforward, I suppose. I think there were crazy moments, sitting at those restaurant tables, when both of us were thinking, Well, why not? We adore each other. We always have. There you are sitting right next to me, and isn't this silly? Why don't I just lean over and give you a kiss? But of course Dan would never have touched me first. I would have to have touched her. Well, neither of us really took those moments seriously at all. But sure, there were moments, there were silences, when I could feel her thinking, Well, here I am sitting on this nice lawn, under this lovely tree, and there's a beautiful apple up there that I've got my eye on, and maybe if I just wait, if I just sit waiting here very quietly, maybe the apple will drop right into my lap. I could feel her thinking it, and I could feel how simple and natural it would be just to do it, just to hold her face and kiss her on the lips, but I never did it. It never happened. So there was me and Aunt Dan in the little house, and then there was me and Aunt Dan not touching each other in all those restaurants, and finally there was one last visit to Aunt Dan just before she died, in her own flat, when she was too sick to touch anybody. (*Music. Aunt Dan's flat.*) There's a nice melody playing on her record-player when I go in. She's smiling. My dress sur-

48

prises her. Well, I thought it would be right to wear a dress. Who is she now? Is she someone I've ever known? I can't tell. Filthy from the train, I go into her bathroom to wash my hands. And in the bathroom there are a thousand things I don't want to see—what pills she takes, what drops, what medicines—with labels I don't want to read—how many, how often to be taken each day. Have there ever been so many things to hide my eyes from in one small room? Soap that has touched her hands, her face; the basin over which she has bent; the well-worn towel, bearer of the imprint of her nose, her mouth—I feel no need now ever to see her again. (*The music has ended. Lemon sits down by Aunt Dan.*) It was the nurse's day off. (*A silence; then to Aunt Dan.*) Er—um—does she clean the flat as well, Aunt Dan? (*A silence.*)

AUNT DAN. She's a wonderful woman. She's been coming here for over a year. I can't tell you. Her kindness . . . She serves me as if she were a nun.

LEMON. A nun?

AUNT DAN. Going to the toilet. My meals. I know her. No secrets. No talking. She hears my thoughts. What would be the point of talking? Lemon, do you know the number of things going on in this room right now? There are hundreds! But while I'm talking, you hear only one—me. It's insanity to live like that. Insane. But she's listening to everything. We listen together. The insects, the wind, the water in the pipes. Sharing these things. Literally *every*thing. The whole world. (*The dark room, as at the beginning of the play.*)

LEMON. (*To the audience.*) There's something that people never say about the Nazis now. (*She drinks.*) By the way, how can anybody like anything better than lime and celery juice? It is the best! The thing is that the Nazis were trying to create a certain way of life for themselves. That's obvious if you read these books I'm reading. They believed that the primitive society of the Germanic tribes had created a life of wholeness and meaning for each person. They blamed the sickness and degeneracy of society as *they* knew it—before they came to power, of course—on the mixture of races that had taken place since that tribal period. In their opinion, all the destructive values of greed, materialism, competitiveness, dishonesty, and so on, had been brought into their society by non-Germanic races.

49

They may have been wrong about it, but that was their belief. So they were trying to create a certain way of life. They were trying to create, or re-create, some sort of society of brothers, bound together by a certain code of loyalty and honor. So to make that attempt, they had to remove the non-Germans, they had to eliminate interbreeding. They were trying to create a certain way of life. Now today, of course, everybody says, "How awful! How awful!" And they were certainly ruthless and thorough in what they did. But the mere fact of killing human beings in order to create a certain way of life is not something that exactly distinguishes the Nazis from everybody else. That's just absurd. When any people feels that its hopes for a desirable future are threatened by some other group, they always do the very same thing. The only question is the degree of the threat. Now for us, for example, criminals are a threat, but they're only a small threat. Right now, we would say about criminals that they're a serious annoyance. We would call them a problem. And right now, the way we deal with that problem is that we take the criminals and we put them in jail. But if these criminals became so vicious, if there got to be so many of them, that our most basic hopes as a society were truly threatened by them — if our whole system of prisons and policemen had fallen so far behind the problem that the streets of our cities were controlled and dominated by violent criminals — then we would find ourselves forgetting the prisons and just killing the criminals instead. It's just a fact. Or let's take the Communists. There are Communists, now, who meet in little groups in America and England. They don't disrupt our entire way of life. They just have their meetings. If they break a law, if they commit a crime, we punish them according to the penalty prescribed. But in some countries, they threaten to destroy their whole way of life. In those countries the Communists are strong, they're violent, they're actually fanatics. And usually it turns out that people decide that they have to be killed. Or when the Europeans first came to America, well, the Indians were there. The Indians fought them for every scrap of land. There was no chance to build the kind of society the Europeans wanted with the Indians there. If they'd tried to put all the Indians in jail, they would have had to put all their effort into building jails, and then, when the Indians came out, they would undoubtedly have started fighting all over again as hard as before. And so they decided to kill the Indians. So it becomes absurd to talk about the Nazis as if the Nazis were unique. That's a kind of hypocrisy. Because the fact is, no society has ever considered the taking of life an unpardonable crime or even, really, a major tragedy. It's something that's done when it has to be done, and it's as simple as that. It's no different from the fact that if I have harmful or obnoxious insects—let's say, cockroaches—living in my house, I probably have to do something about it. Or at least, the question I have to ask is: How many are there? If the cockroaches are small, and I see a few of them now and then, that may not be very disturbing to me. But if I see big ones, if I start to see them often, then I say to myself, they have to be killed. Now some people simply hate to kill cockroaches, so they'll wait much longer. But if the time comes when there are hundreds of them, when they're crawling out of every drawer, when they're in the oven, when they're in the refrigerator, when they're in the toilet, when they're in the bed, then even the person who hates to kill them will go to the shop and get some poison and start killing, because the way of life that that person had wanted to lead is now really being threatened. Yes, the fact is, it is very unpleasant to kill another creature—let's admit it. Each one of us has his own fear of pain and his own fear of death. It's true for people and for every type of creature that lives. I remember once squashing a huge brown roach—I slammed it with my shoe, but it wasn't dead and I sat and watched it, and it's an awful period just before any creature dies—any insect or animal—when you're watching the stupid, ignorant things that that creature is trying to do to fight off its death—whether it's moving its arms or its legs, or it's kicking, or it's trying to crawl to another part of the floor, or it's trying to lift itself off the ground—those things can't prevent death!—but the creature is trying out every gesture it's capable of, hoping, hoping that something will help it. And I remember how I felt as I watched that big brown roach squirming and crawling, and yet it was totally squashed, and I could see its insides slowly come oozing out. And I'm sure that the bigger a thing is, the more you hate to see it. I remember when I was in school we did some experiments on these big rats, and we had to inject them with poison and watch them die—and, of course, no matter what hu-

51

mane method you use in any laboratory to kill the animals, there's a moment that comes when they sense what's happening and they start to try out all those telltale squirming gestures. And with people, of course, it's the same thing. The bigger the creature, the harder it is to kill. We know it takes at least ten minutes to hang a person. Even if you shoot them in the head, it's not instantaneous — they still make those squirming movements at least for a moment. And people in gas chambers rush to the doors that they know very well are firmly locked. They fight each other to get to the doors. So killing is always very unpleasant. Now when people say, "Oh the Nazis were different from anyone, the Nazis were different from anyone," well, perhaps that's true in at least one way, which is that they observed themselves extremely frankly in the act of killing, and they admitted frankly how they really felt about the whole process. Yes, of course, they admitted, it's very unpleasant, and if we didn't have to do it in order to create a way of life that we want for ourselves, we would never be involved in killing at all. But since we have to do it, why not be truthful about it, and why not admit that yes, yes, there's something inside us that likes to kill. Some part of us. There's something inside us that likes to do it. Why shouldn't that be so? Our human nature is derived from the nature of different animals, and of course there's a part of animal nature that likes to kill. If killing were totally repugnant to animals, they couldn't survive. So an enjoyment of killing is somewhere inside us, somewhere in our nature. In polite society, people don't discuss it, but the fact is that it's enjoyable — it's enjoyable — to make plans for killing, and it's enjoyable to learn about killing that is done by other people, and it's enjoyable to think about killing, and it's enjoyable to read about killing, and it's even enjoyable actually to kill, although when we ourselves are actually killing, an element of unpleasantness always comes in. That unpleasant feeling starts to come in. But even there, one has to say, even though there's an unpleasant side at first to watching people die, we have to admit that after watching for a while — maybe after watching for a day or maybe for a week or a year — it's still in a way unpleasant to watch, but on the other hand we have to admit that after we've watched it for all that time — well, we don't really actually care any more. We have to admit that we don't really care. And I think that that last admission is what really makes people go mad about the Nazis, because in our own society we have this kind of cult built up around what people call the feeling of "compassion." I remember my mother screaming all the time, "Compassion! Compassion! You have to have compassion for other people! You have to have compassion for other human beings!" And I must admit, there's something I find refreshing about the Nazis, which is partly why I enjoy reading about them every night, because they sort of had the nerve to say, "Well, what *is* this compassion? Because I don't really know what it is. So I want to know, really, what is it?" And they must have sort of asked each other at some point, "Well say, Heinz, have *you* ever felt it?" "Well no, Rolf, what about you?" And they all had to admit that they really didn't know what the hell it was. And I find it sort of relaxing to read about those people, because I have to admit that I don't know either. I mean, I think I've felt it reading a novel, and I think I've felt it watching a film — "Oh how sad, that child is sick! That mother is crying!" — but I can't ever remember feeling it in life. I just don't remember feeling it about something that was happening in front of my eyes. And I can't believe that other people are that different from me. In other words, it was unpleasant to watch that pitiful roach scuttling around on my floor dying, but I can't say I really felt *sad* about it. I felt revolted or sickened, I guess I would say, but I can't say that I really felt sorry for the roach. And plenty of people have cried in my presence or seemed to be suffering, and I remember wishing they'd *stop* suffering and *stop* crying and leave me alone, but I don't remember, frankly, that I actually cared. So you have to say finally, well, fine, if there are all these people like my mother who want to go around talking about compassion all day, well, fine, that's their right. But it's sort of refreshing to admit every once in a while that they're talking about something that possibly doesn't exist. And it's sort of an ambition of mine to go around some day and ask each person I meet, Well here is something you've heard about to the point of nausea all of your life, but do you personally, actually remember feeling it, and if you really do, could you please describe the particular circumstances in which you felt it and what it actually felt *like*? Because if there's one thing I learned from Aunt Dan, I suppose you could say it was a

53

kind of honesty. It's easy to say we should all be loving and sweet, but meanwhile we're enjoying a certain way of life — and we're actually *living* — due to the existence of certain other people who are willing to take the job of killing on their own backs, and it's not a bad thing every once in a while to admit that that's the way we're living, and even to give to those certain people a tiny, fractional crumb of thanks. You can be very sure that it's more than they expect, but I think they'd be grateful, all the same. (*The lights fade as she sits and drinks.*)

NOTE ON THE TEXT

The foregoing text of AUNT DAN AND LEMON represents everything I, as the author, really know about the
characters and the story. My real preference would be to leave
it at that and let the audience make of it what they will. But in
the New York production it was decided that it would help the
audience to spell out a few points, and if you are putting on this
play and are beginning to get the feeling that your audience
might need some assistance, you could also add the lines we
added. Before Aunt Dan's sickbed scene, before Lemon tells the
audience "It was the nurse's day off" we had Lemon say, "Aunt
Dan had completely changed. She wasn't herself." Then, after
Aunt Dan finishes that scene by saying "Literally *every*thing.
The whole world," we had Lemon tell the audience, "I didn't
understand a single word. Aunt Dan would never have anything to say to me again, and so my education had been completed. I was on my own." And then she returned to her London
flat and continued, "You know, there's something people never
say about the Nazis now." (If you want to make it *even clearer* that
the subject of the play is the education of Lemon and that
Lemon's final monologue represents her amplification of what
she has learned [or thinks she has learned] from Aunt Dan, then
you could drop the line "I was on my own," which represents a
separate thought, and Lemon could say simply, "I didn't understand a single word. Aunt Dan would never have anything to
say to me again. My education had been completed. You know,
there's something people never say about the Nazis now.") We
also felt, in the London production, that the audience was
becoming truly lost in the Mindy-Raimondo sequence, because
they could see absolutely no connection between that sequence
and any issue that had previously been raised in the play—at
least until the final moment of the sequence—and so we decided
to reveal that this sequence, too, would have to do with the previously much-discussed theme of killing. The scene before the
scene at Morley's was therefore changed as follows:

MINDY. (*To Freddie.*) All right, I'll do it. Sure. Why not. But
you're giving me the money now, right?

FREDDIE. Well, I'm giving you part of it. You'll get the rest when the bastard is dead. Flora and I will bring him into Morley's tomorrow evening at nine o'clock. We'll work it out so that when we come in, you'll already be there, with a date. And we'll call you Rosa.

MINDY. Okay, Freddie. Whatever you like.

Many people felt that the relation of the Mindy sequence to the play was clarified by this change. The audience was able to observe more consciously Mindy's skill at manipulation, the quality Aunt Dan so admires. I myself still think it's possible that the shock of the murder is a very important element of the play, however, so I think my original version may still be worth trying.

Simply to prevent the play from growing too long, the London and New York productions cut Aunt Dan's monologue "Well, the telephone thing we worked out was great." (Lemon's line about watching the wind in Aunt Dan's hair was cut, and in its place she said "And then, as we were talking, night would fall." So after Aunt Dan's line, "Phyllis would serve these gigantic salads out on the grass" Lemon said, "Her friends were the best. Especially the people she'd known when she was young and wild and living in London.") What is lost by cutting this monologue, though, is that this is the only time we get to see Aunt Dan herself directly involved in a game of deceit and trickery; in the rest of the play we hear her telling Lemon about what *others* have done.

In the London and New York productions, the Morley's scenes took place at a bar, not a restaurant table, and at certain moments loud laughter and a couple of lines could be heard from the corner of the bar where Freddie, Marty, and Flora were gathered. At one point Marty said, "So I pushed his head into a bowl of potato chips! Ha ha ha— And you know, it made the most wonderful sound! Ha ha ha—" And just before Mindy said to Raimondo "Say—it looks like Marty is flirting with your date!" Flora had said to Marty and Freddie, "So I said 'Is that a new method of contraception?'" and Marty and Freddie had laughed wildly.

To streamline the play further—to avoid the danger that the audience would become impatient or bored—we chose to have two Kissinger discussions between Aunt Dan and Mother rather than three. If you want to do this also, Mindy's two garden monologues have to be run together, so that after the line "But Andy was always so sweet to me," Mindy should continue, "You know, it would be late at night . . ." The Aunt Dan—Mother sequence which begins "Susie, look, he has to make a choice" is thus cut. What is lost in making this cut is Aunt Dan's explanation of her belief that the policies she favors are ultimately grounded in a quest for world peace. If the cut is made, her argument therefore seems to that degree less rational, less defensible, and more purely an expression of psychological impulses. Also, I think the feeling of the endlessly alternating days and nights of Lemon's memory is quite important, and this can't quite be felt if the cut is made.

Max Stafford-Clark felt the audience should know a bit more about the Mother, so the speech dealing with Mother's meeting Aunt Dan was expanded to include an introductory section about Mother's life at Oxford (page 18). Personally, I feel that the short version of the speech can convey a great deal, and it moves the play along faster. The short version would begin: "During my very first winter in Oxford I discovered a wonderful huge meadow near the edge of town where I used to take walks" and it would continue as it is.

After Aunt Dan speaks about love (page 47), the audience probably is most interested in what happened to Lemon and Aunt Dan, so in London there was sometimes a sort of sigh of impatience when Lemon referred to a character from an earlier part of the play, the Father. So the decision was made to cut the passage from "My father didn't know about my mother's conversations" through "And it didn't bother him." I've left the passage in because I think it completes that part of the story.

In the second New York production, Aunt Dan's description of her nurse was re-written to clarify the point that Aunt Dan has lost her obsession with maintaining control over her environment and is now in a condition to share her life with another person—to value that person's kindness and receive her love:

LEMON. I feel no need now ever to see her again. Aunt Dan had completely changed. She wasn't herself. It was the nurse's day off. (*A silence.*) (*To Aunt Dan.*) Er—um—does she clean the flat as well, Aunt Dan? (*A silence.*)

AUNT DAN. She's a wonderful woman. She's been coming here for over a year. Six mornings a week, walking in at dawn. Hanging up her coat. So gentle. I can't tell you—her kindness—she serves me as if she were a nun.

LEMON. A nun?

AUNT DAN. Going to the toilet. My meals. Making my bed. At first I said, I can't stand this. These days, endless days, days of nothing, and this person always there, watching me. (*Pause.*) When she first came, I talked all the time—I told her everything. And then one day, in the middle of a sentence, she sat down beside me very suddenly, and I stopped talking, and all at once I could hear all these things that were happening in the room—the insects buzzing and the curtains bumping against the window and the water in the pipes—hundreds of things— (*Pause.*) Sometimes we don't say a word all day. Just sharing these things. Literally *everything*. The whole world.

LEMON. (*To the audience.*) I didn't understand a single word.

I must admit, I still like the old version.

Finally, for reasons of length, in the last monologue we cut the section about Communists beginning with "Or let's take the Communists" and ending "they have to be killed."

NOTE ON THE SET

AUNT DAN AND LEMON is a very hard play to design. It has an awful lot of scenes and an awful lot of requirements. The author — trusting in the genius of designers and directors — has cavalierly called for beds, tables, chairs, and whole rooms to magically appear and disappear without interrupting the flow of the action. Moreover, the requirement which is perhaps most important is never mentioned in the text, namely that the setting must help the audience to understand the play. Specifically, let's face it — the play is made up of a series of short fragments, including Lemon's stories of Aunt Dan, Aunt Dan's stories of Mindy, and Mindy's story of people like Raimondo and Freddie whom Aunt Dan herself never met, and so the danger exists that the evening will seem like a sequence of fifty completely unrelated one-act plays. The set can be very, very important in helping the audience to see it instead as a unified event, a single story. The unifying theme of the play is clearly the education of Lemon, and the set can help us to understand that. On the other hand, it is desirable for the set to allow each of the fragments to have its own individual identity and color. The play can be seen from a formal point of view as a sort of battle of clashing elements and contrasting styles, and this means that there must be elements of surprise and variety as well as unity in the scenic presentation.

In the Max Stafford-Clark production, designed by Peter Hartwell, which was done at the Royal Court Theatre in London and Joseph Papp's Public Theater in New York, there was a sort of painted garden in which the play took place, made up of flats and wings and a painted false proscenium, and a revolve was used to help transport all the various elements to their proper places without interrupting the play.

At one point, when we were discussing what the set might be, the possibility was raised of building a permanent, unchanging garden set, with real grass and flowers, and doing even the scenes with Mindy, Raimondo, and so on using garden furniture. Ultimately we decided that this would not give enough scenic support to the Mindy scenes, nor would it allow them to provide a sharp stylistic contrast to the rest of the play. And so we chose instead to have a series of sets which — with different degrees of detail — illustrated the various locations of the play. The family dinner table was just a table which appeared out of the darkness. Lemon's little house was large, detailed, and realistic — a real little house (or two walls of one, anyway) which came out on the revolve to face the audience, complete with bed, window-seat, and Lemon's treasured possessions. (The scenes in the little house are perhaps the most difficult in the play, and strict realism is of course only one possible approach to making them work.) Andy's flat, Mindy's flat, and Morley's were done very simply, but they filled the whole stage; they were complete sets, made up of a few pieces which flew in from above or were slid in from the sides or were carried in by stage-hands. In the scene in Mindy's bedroom, the back flat parted at one point, and the whole garden could be seen, with Aunt Dan and Lemon in it, watching. The entire floor of the set was a black carpet, which served as a kind of menacing black grass in the garden scenes.

When we first started performing the play, we used a series of front-cloths to mask the appearance of the stage-hands, but after a while we decided that this was more distracting than allowing the stage-hands to do their work in full view at certain moments while the actors went on with the play.

It is obviously enormously important that the audience should understand — not just intellectually but also emotionally — that the Mindy scenes are stories Aunt Dan tells Lemon in the little house (and that they amplify the attitudes she has previously revealed herself to have about political matters). When we changed casts in New York, Max Stafford-Clark re-staged the scene in Andy's flat right in the little house, with Andy, June, Mindy, and Jasper joining Aunt Dan and Lemon there. (In Max Stafford-Clark's staging, Lemon appeared in every scene, although she and Aunt Dan were hidden at the beginning of the scene in Mindy's bedroom.) It was suggested that perhaps a way could be devised for the little house — and Lemon's bed — to be used for the scene in Mindy's bedroom as well, although we never actually managed to do this.

If one approach to the play would be to center it all on the little house, another would of course be to center it on Lemon's current London flat, which is where the text says the play "really" takes place.

PROPERTY LIST

Armchair
Table
Sheets of paper
Brandy
Glasses
Napkin
Pieces of rope
Bed (with knobs at head and foot)

When I was around thirteen, I was sitting on a sofa with an older woman, and she said to me rather fiercely, "You don't understand this now, but when you get older, you'll come to appreciate the importance of comfort." This did turn out to be true. At that time I really didn't have much to be comforted about or comforted from, so naturally comfort didn't matter to me then. And now it does. And the older I get, the more I long to feel really comfortable. But I've also come to realize that an awful lot of preparatory work must be undertaken before that particular feeling can begin to exist, and I've learned, too, how all that effort can count for nothing if even one tiny element of the world around me refuses to fit into its necessary place. Yes, I'm at home in my lovely apartment, I'm sitting in my cozy rocking chair, there are flowers on the table, tranquil colors of paint on the walls. But if I've caught a fever and I'm feeling sick, or if a nearby faucet has developed a leak, or if a dog in the courtyard six floors below me is barking, the unity of my peaceful scene is spoiled, and comfort flies out the window. And unfortunately, what in fact prevents me more than anything else from feeling really comfortable — whether I'm leaning back against a soft banquette in a pleasant restaurant or spending a drowsy morning in bed propped up on three or four pillows — is actually the well-intentioned ethical training I received as a child.

My parents brought me up to believe that there was something terribly important called morality — an approach towards life which was based on the paradoxical concept of self-restraint (or the restraint of one part of the self by another part). Instead of teaching me merely to be alert to the threat of potential enemies outside myself, I was instructed to practice, in addition, a sort of constant vigilance over my own impulses — even, at times, a subjugation of them, when certain abstract criteria of justice (which lived in my own mind) determined that someone else's interests should be allowed to prevail over my own desires. Morality, this fantastic and complicated system (which a good many of my friends were taught by their parents as well), was, as we first encountered it, a set of principles and laws. But these principles and laws were really nothing more than a description of how a person would behave if he cared equally about all human beings, even though one of them happened, in fact, to be himself—if he cared about them equally and deeply, so that their suffering actually caused him to suffer as well. And there were such people—there were people who experienced a sense of awe, of humility, before the miracle of life—people who had a gift for morality the way some people had a gift for music or pleasure. But we, for the most part, lacked that gift, so we were taught laws and principles, the simplest of which was just that each other person was as real as we were. Almost all of the rest of morality followed from that. If I could learn to believe that someone, a stranger, was just as real as I was, I could easily see how badly it would hurt him if I treated him cruelly, if I lied to him, if I betrayed him.

But the world is in a constant turmoil of conflict and struggle, I learned, and so morality was not merely a way of looking at life; it was also a guide to action. And its teaching in regard to action was that I should love all the people in the world equally, and that I should take the action prompted by that love. Of course, I myself was one of those people, and in saying that all people should be equally loved, morality was also saying that I, too, like others, had a rightful place in the world, and so in following the teachings of morality I might even find myself at times acting in defense of my own interests. I might even find myself fighting or killing in their defense. But this would only be so if I had first stepped outside myself, if I had approached myself as merely one among all the human creatures on the earth for whom I cared, and if I, out of my equal love, had solemnly decided to send myself into battle on the side of myself, because this was necessary for everyone's sake.

My daily obligation, then, was certainly not to refrain from action. On the contrary, passivity was seen, from this point of view, as merely a lazy, indifferent, and cowardly form of actionless action. Nor was my obligation to refrain from all activity on my own behalf. No, my daily obligation was, first and foremost, to learn how to make a correct and careful study of the world.

Perhaps I had long ago rejected self-love and self-interest as guides to action. Perhaps I had sworn to myself that I would always act only for everyone's sake, out of love for everyone.

But if I didn't know what the world was like, how could I know what action to take? Perhaps it was permissible to kill a person in order to prevent a terrible evil. But if I acted impulsively, heedlessly, and blindly — if I killed the wrong person because I relied on an erroneous suspicion or an intuition, or I based my action on some erroneous theory of the world which I'd accepted for years because it happened to be flattering to someone like me — would I still have behaved in a permissible way? Obviously not. How, then, could I act at all unless, for a moment, for an hour, for a day, I had ruthlessly stripped from my mind all those prejudices and preconceptions which my own particular situation and my own particular history had forced upon me — unless I had cast all these from me and looked at the world for what it was? Who really threatened me? Who really threatened you? What would be the effect on me if you did this? What would be the effect on you if I did that? I had to learn how to examine the world and then to re-examine it, because it changed very fast. And so it turned out that morality insisted upon accuracy — perpetual, painstaking study and research.

I realize now that this entire training in morality is a jarring element in the life I'm leading, and in my struggle to feel comfortable, to feel at ease, it functions rather like a dog whose barking never stops, a dog whose barking persists throughout the day and then continues regularly all night long. It is a perpetual irritation. Everything visible around me may be perfect and serene, but inside, there is this voice which never stops denouncing me. It does not fit in. Of course I'd be pleased if I could claim that all my relations with other people were in perfect harmony with the laws of morality — and as a matter of fact, in my daily interactions with my friends and colleagues and loved ones, I usually try to follow ethical precepts. But when I draw the curtains of perception a little bit wider and consider the fact that there are thousands and millions of people in the world, all quite real, and that I have some sort of relation to every one of them, I have to admit that it would be hard to insist that all these relations of mine are truly obedient to those solemn laws. I'll say this much — if my relation to each and every peasant in Cambodia is indeed exactly what the principles of morality would demand it to be, it's a miraculous coincidence, because it takes a lot of effort to behave correctly in regard to my friends, and from one end of the year to another I never give those peasants a single thought.

The point I'm making is quite simple. It's that each year I do a certain amount of labor (I personally happen to do something—acting in films—which I find quite amusing), and I'm paid a certain sum of money, and I spend it in certain ways. When I receive my paycheck for the week, I immediately employ groups of people to start making me things, like coffee-grinders and light bulbs and recordings of great violinists, and streams of goods start flowing in my direction from all over the world. In contrast to this, as everyone knows, when a gold miner in South Africa receives the payment for his week's work, he can only set in motion, say, one one-thousandth of that much activity, most of it strictly in the agricultural sector. But even after I've done all the buying that I'm planning to do, half of my money still remains, and I then spend most of that on employing people to do services for me. With some of the money I employ a woman to come on Wednesday morning and clean my apartment, and with most of it I pay the government of my country, the United States of America, to perform a similar service in regard to my environment as a whole. And, of course, one of the most important tasks which my government undertakes is to try to preserve the international structure of the world more or less as it is, so that next year it will not suddenly be I who is working a seventy-hour week in some Godforsaken pit or digging in some field under the burning sun.

Now, as governments go, as governments have gone throughout the course of history, mine has much to recommend it, in my opinion. My view is absolutely that United States society, within its own borders, is less oppressive and less brutal than most, and if given complete sway over the entire world, a United States tyranny would be preferable to many. But as my government happens to be the representative through which I personally conduct my relationships with most of my fellow human beings, I'm obliged to ask, for as long as I continue to be bound by my childhood training, whether my govenment's actions conform to the laws of morality. Of course, people often say that governments, when dealing with international relations, cannot possibly be responsive to these laws, which appropriately apply only to private life and a government's domestic sphere. The explanation they give is that any government which tried to follow such laws would be at a great disadvantage, because the world's other governments would continue to ignore them. And it is often said, also, that governments have obligations to the people of their own countries, but not to the people of other countries. But, really, to argue in this way is to consider governments to be somehow living beings in their own right, with their own special habits and obligations, whereas from the point of view of the principles of morality, governments are simply organizations established for the convenience of those who control them; they are mere intermediaries, the bearers of messages.

My fellow citizens and I may very well be surrounded by immoral enemies, and we may be tempted to take utterly ruthless actions against them. We may well feel a profound attachment to one another, combined with a cool indifference towards everyone else on the globe. But the principles of morality do not waver in the face of our particular circumstances; they demand obedience whether obedience is difficult or easy. They rarely insist that a group of people should allow themselves to be trampled upon or destroyed. But they do reject the opinion that those near to me should be treated with love, while those who are distant may be treated with contempt. And they do judge my actions with the same severity whether I perform them with my own hands or through instrumentalities or chains of command. And so of course they do judge my government's actions, and they find that, although I may be a friendly fellow to meet on the street, I have found, through my government, a sneaky way to do some terrible things.

Of course, it is certainly the case that there are crimes which I do not commit against the world's human beings. My boot does not oppress the peoples of Poland or Hungary. The prisoners in the jails of my country are not hung upside down and tortured; our poor do not die of cholera or plague. But my relation to most of the people in the world just cannot be described as exactly the one which morality would demand. And this is why I realize that as long as I preserve my loyalty to my childhood training I will never know what it is to be truly comfortable, and this is why I feel a fantastic need to tear that training out of my heart once and for all so that I can finally begin to enjoy the life that is spread out before me like a feast. And every time a friend makes that happy choice and sets himself free, I find that I inwardly exult and rejoice, because it means there will be one less person to disapprove of me if I choose to do the same.

As I write these words, in New York City in 1985, more and more people who grew up around me are making this decision; they are throwing away their moral chains and learning to enjoy their true situation: Yes, they are admitting loudly and bravely, we live in beautiful homes, we're surrounded by beautiful gardens, our children are playing with wonderful toys, and our kitchen shelves are filled with wonderful food. And if there are people out there who don't seem to like us and who would like to break into our homes and take what we have, well then, part of our good fortune is that we can afford to pay guards to man our gates and keep those people away. And if those who protect us need to hit people in the face with the butts of their rifles, or if they need perhaps even to turn around and shoot, they have our permission, and we only hope they'll do what they do with diligence and skill.

The amazing thing I've noticed about those friends of mine who've made that choice is that as soon as they've made it, they begin to blossom, to flower, because they are no longer hiding, from themselves or anyone else, the true facts about their own lives. They become very frank about human nature. They freely admit that man is a predatory creature, a hunter and a fighter, and they admit that it can warm a human's heart to trick an enemy, to make him cry, to make him do what he doesn't want to do, and even to make him crawl in the mud and die in agony. They admit that to manipulate people can be an art, and that to deceive people can be entertaining. They admit that there's a skill involved in playing life's game, and they admit that it's exciting to bully and threaten and outwit and defeat all the other people who are playing against you. And as they learn to admit these things, and they lose the habit of looking over their shoulders in fear at what exists in their own souls, they develop the charm and grace which shine out from all people who are truly comfortable with themselves, who are not worried, who are not ashamed of their own actions. These are people who are free to love life exuberantly. They can enjoy a bottle of wine or a walk in the garden with unmixed pleasure, because they feel justified in having the bottle of wine, in having the garden. And if, by chance, they run into the laundress who takes care of their clothes, they can chat with her happily and easily, because they accept the fact that some people, themselves, happen to wear beautiful clothes, and others are paid to keep them clean. And, in fact, these people who accept themselves are people whose company everyone enjoys.

So there are those who live gracelessly in a state of discomfort, because they allow themselves to be whipped on an hourly basis by morality's lash, and then there's another group of cheerful, self-confident people who've put morality aside for now, and they're looking happy. But whenever I start dreaming about self-confident people I begin to get terribly nervous, because I always think of the marvelous self-confidence of Hitler, the way he would expound his theories of the world to his aides and orderlies and secretaries at the dining room table night after night with no sense that he needed to keep checking to see if his theories were really true. Hitler's boundless self-confidence enabled him to live each day as a tireless murderer; no weakness, no flagging energy, kept his knife from plunging into his victims hour after hour with mechanical ease. And so, naturally, I ask myself, will I become like him? Yes, of course, I long to be comfortable. But to become a murderer? To murder everyone? If I gave up morality, what would prevent me from murdering everyone?

Hitler was a man who was drawn to murder, to thinking about murder, to dwelling on murder. Particularly to dwelling on murder. Can we not imagine with what eager excitement he must have listened to all of the latest reports from the death camps, the crematoria, which he never in fact visited on a single occasion? But when we speak of dwelling on murder . . . that person standing over the daily newspaper—reading about the massacre, reading about the bloodbath, reading about the execution in a room in the prison—that person is me. And am I not in some part of myself identifying with the one in the story who is firing the machine gun at the innocent people, who is pulling the switch that sends the jolts of power through the prisoner strapped in the electric chair? And do I not also enjoy reading about those incredible scientists who are making the preparations for what we might do in some future war that might take place? Do I not join them in picturing, with some small relish, the amazing effects which our different devices would have on possible victims? Is my blood not racing with abnormal speed as I read about these things? Is there not something trembling inside me? I know that these planners, these scientists, are not involved in killing. They're killing no one. But I see what they're doing — they're building the gas chambers, getting together the pellets of poison, assembling the rooms where the clothing and valuables will all be sorted, transporting the victims to convenient camps, and asking them to get undressed for the showers and disinfection which will soon be following. Of course, no one is putting people into the chambers. No one is pumping in the gas.

But wait a minute. Am I crazy now? What am I saying? What do I have to do with Hitler? Of course, I may have insane impulses somewhere inside me, but the difference between Hitler and me is that there was nothing in Hitler which restrained him from following any of his insane impulses to their logical, insane conclusions — he was capable of doing anything at all, if given the chance — because he was utterly without connection to morality.

But I just was thinking about cutting my connection to morality also.

Yes, I was thinking about it. But I didn't do it. At least, I have no memory of doing it. Or was there actually some moment when I did do it, which I've now forgotten?

I don't seem to remember what's happened at all. I know there was a time when I was not like Hitler.

The past feels so terribly close. It's as if I could reach out and touch it. Could I have become like one of those people who remembers, as if it were yesterday, the time when principles of decency grew freshly in his heart, when a love for humanity set him off on his path in life, who still believes that each of his actions is driven and motivated by those very principles and that very love, but who in fact is a coarse and limited brute who buried both love and principles long ago?

How could a person break his attachment to morality without noticing it, without feeling it, without remembering it? Could a perfectly decent person just turn into a cold-hearted beast, a monster, and still feel pretty much the same?

Of course. A perfectly decent person can turn into a monster perfectly easily. And there's no reason why he would feel any different. Because the difference between a perfectly decent person and a monster is just a few thoughts. The perfectly decent person who follows a certain chain of reasoning, ever so slightly and subtly incorrect, becomes a perfect monster at the end of the chain.

Thoughts have extraordinary power in the human world. They can do odd things. Familiar thoughts can lead us by the hand to very strange thoughts. And in a way, we're not as clever as our own thoughts, which have a peculiar habit of developing on their own and taking us to conclusions we never particularly wanted to reach. Even within each thought, other thoughts are hidden, waiting to crawl out.

As the morning begins and I slowly turn my head to look at the clock on my beside bookcase, my thoughts are already leaping and playing in my brain, ceaselessly spawning other thoughts, changing their shape, dividing in two and then dividing again, merging, dancing together in gigantic clumps. There's no end to the things that the thoughts will do if no one is paying any attention to them.

Our thoughts jump and fly through the pathways of our minds. The world races forward. And meanwhile we're walking slowly around in a daze, trying to remember whether we're still connected to morality or not. False arguments, rapidly expressed, confuse us, seduce us, corrupt us. The chains of reasoning, of thinking, appeared to be sound. What was wrong? But we forget that thinking has its own pathology, and we sit in some room listening to a discussion, and something reasonable and admirable is said, and we nod our heads, and somehow we keep on nodding, and moments later we've agreed to something which would make our former selves turn purple with shame. But we sit there blankly, unaware that anything has happened. Why was it that we failed to notice the first signs of sickness in the argument? At the crucial moment, had our attention wandered? Why would that be? Are we particularly tired right now? Exhausted?

These are the things that happen to us every day. They may happen to you as you read the play you're holding in your hand.

And the characters in the play, like you and me, are formed by the chains of reasoning they've followed.

Our lives develop, and our thoughts change, and as our thoughts change, we change. We change each day in small steps, brief conversations, half-conscious moments of reflection, of doubt and resolution.

I stand at the door of my house, ready to defend the loved ones inside from the marauder lurking in the dark. As I steel myself to shoot the marauder, I say to myself, "I must be hard. Cold. Unsentimental." I repeat the litany a hundred times. And the next morning, when the marauder has not come — or the marauder has come and I have shot him — what do I do with my litany? It doesn't disappear from my mind merely because there is no marauder any more. Will I adopt it as a creed? Will I decide to believe that unsentimentality is an important virtue? Will I start to take pleasure in my own coldness? Will I teach myself to be hard now in situations where hardness once would have seemed like a crime?

A friend describes to me the pleasure he took in hitting someone who had insulted him, and I realize that I, too, take pleasure in his story. I recognize in myself a desire for revenge against every person who has ever hurt me. He tells me that he finds it hypocritical to deny that the desire for revenge exists in our hearts. I agree entirely. Will I now decide to adopt revenge as a legitimate motive for my daily actions?

I meet a young woman at a quiet dinner party, and as we sit together she tells me that she sometimes likes to go out with gangsters. She describes in detail the techniques they use in getting other people to do what they want — bribery, violence. I'm shocked and repelled by the stories she tells. A few months later I run into her again at another party and I hear more stories, and this time I don't feel shocked. I'm no longer so aware of the sufferings of those whom the gangsters confront. I'm more impressed by the high style and shrewdness of the gangsters themselves. I begin to understand how difficult it is to be a successful gangster and what extraordinary skill is in fact required to climb to the top of a gangster empire. I find myself listening with a certain enjoyment. By the third time that I encounter this woman I've become a connoisseur of gangster techniques, and the stories she tells now strike me as funny. I consider myself to be, as I always was, a person who entirely disapproves of gangsters, but I still pass on to a friend of mine some of the best stories in the spirit of fun. If my friend now objects that the stories are not really funny, will I find myself somewhat annoyed? Will my friend now seem to me narrow-minded — a humorless prude?

And so every day we encounter the numberless insidious intellectual ploys by which the principle of immorality makes a plausible case for itself, and for every ploy there is a corresponding weakness in our own thinking which causes us not to notice where we're being led until we've already fallen into the trap. Unfortunately, these small intellectual infirmities of ours — our brief lapses of concentration, our susceptibility to slightly inappropriate analogies, the way we tend to forget in what particular contexts the ideas in our heads first made their appearance there, the way our attention can be drawn at the wrong moment by the magician's patter to the hand which does not contain the mysterious coin — just happen to have the power to send history racing off down a path of horror. Morality, if it survived, could protect us from horror, but very little protects morality. And morality, besides, is hard to protect, because morality is only a few thoughts in our heads. And just as we quickly grow accustomed to brutal deeds and make way before them, so we are quickly stunned into foggy submission by the brutal thoughts which, in our striving for comfort, we have allowed into our minds and which can snuff the life out of morality in a matter of moments if we happen to look the other way. And all the time we are operating under the illusion that we, mere individuals, have no power at all over the course of history, when that is in fact (for better or worse) the very opposite of the case.

The shocking truth is that history, too, is at the mercy of my thoughts, and the political leaders of the world sit by their radios waiting to hear whether morality has sickened or died inside my skull. The process is simple. I speak with you, and then I turn out the light and I go to sleep, but, while I sleep, you talk on the telephone to a man you met last year in Ohio, and you tell him what I said, and he hangs up and talks to a neighbor of his, and what I said keeps travelling, farther and farther. And just as a fly can quite blithely and indifferently land on the nose of a queen, so the thought which you mentioned to the man in Ohio can make its way with unimaginable speed into the mind of a president. Because a society is very little more than a network of brains, and a president is no less involved in his society's network than anyone else, and there is almost nothing that he thinks that doesn't come right from that network. In fact, he is virtually incapable of coming up with an attitude to any problem or to any event which has not been nurtured and developed in that network of brains. So as he searches in his mind for a sound approach to the latest cable from the Soviet Premier, what comes to the surface is a thought which he happened to get from me, a thought, perhaps, which first occurred to me some evening thirty years ago when my grandmother turned over a card in a game of canasta with a certain unusual expression on her face.

My grandmother's silence, her manner, affected me. Her gesture, expressive of certain feelings about myself, gave rise in me to a thought, and that thought had nothing to do with the Soviet Union. It was just a thought about daily life. But when it sooner or later becomes necessary for any of us — whether president or ordinary citizen — to come up with thoughts about political affairs, the only raw materials which we have to draw on are the thoughts we've previously formed on the conflicts and dramas of daily life. Our thoughts may be ones we've dreamed up ourselves, or we may have acquired them from our parents, from our lovers, from our Aunt Dan, or from the man in Ohio. But wherever we've found them, they are all we have to work with. Our political attitudes can only come out of what we are — what we were as children, what we've become today, what we've learned in school, at the playground, at the party, at the beach, at home, in bed. And as all of our attitudes flow into action, flow into history, the bedroom and the battlefield soon seem to be one.

My political opinions fly out across the world and determine the course of political events. And political events are determined as well by what I think about the conversation I had with my mother last Saturday when we were having tea. What I say to you about my neighbor's child affects what you feel about the nurse who sits by the side of your friend in the hospital room, and what you say about the nurse affects what your friend's sister thinks about the government of China. Everything you are affects me, and everything I am, all my thoughts — the behavior I admire or criticize, the way I choose to spend an hour of my time, the things I like to talk about, the stories I like to hear, the jokes I like to tell, the events which delight me and the events which displease me — affect the course of history whether I like it or not, whether I know about it or not, whether I care or not. My power over history is inescapable except through death. Privacy is an illusion. What I do is public, and what I think is public. The fragility of my own thoughts becomes the fragility of the world. The ease with which I could become a swine is the ease with which the world could fall apart, like something rotten.

The uncomfortable and incompetent slaves of morality — those awkward, crippled creatures who insist on believing in a standard which condemns them — are less admirable only than those few perfect beings who perhaps obey morality completely. There are a million possible degrees of obedience, and the person who obeys morality to a higher degree is more admirable than the person who obeys it less, and the person who doesn't struggle to obey it at all is not admirable at all. Of course, almost everyone describes himself as a servant of morality, and even the most outrageous criminals will make such claims, not just publicly but even to themselves, and undoubtedly Hitler himself was no exception. In fact, there is no action so manifestly evil that it cannot be seen and described as a justifiable and purely defensive measure. But none of this should be allowed to confuse us. And it is true also that if we ourselves have any sympathy or any affection for people — if we like people — we will be fond of many who treat morality with utter indifference, including people whose personal histories make their indifference most understandable. But this should not be allowed to confuse us either. Morality happens to be a protection which we need in order to avoid total historical disaster, and so we are obliged to maintain a constant, precise awareness of how morality is faring in the world. Unfortunately or not, we cannot afford to turn our eyes away when our acquaintances, our friends, or we ourselves, drop down a few degrees on the scale of obedience to moral principles. It is obviously foolish and absurd to judge some small decline on the moral scale as if it were a precipitous, lengthy slide. But the temptation is great to be easy on ourselves, and we've all discovered that it's easier to be easy on ourselves if we're all easy on each other too, and so we are. So when a precipitous slide really does take place, a particular effort is required in order to see it. Sophistries, false chains of reasoning, deception, and self-deception all rush in to conceal the fact that any change has occurred at all.

If we live from day to day without self-examination, we remain unaware of the dangers we may pose to ourselves and the world. But if we look into the mirror, we just might observe a rapacious face. Perhaps the face will even show subtle traces, here and there, of hatred and savagery beneath the surface. And maybe most of us look a little bit like Hitler, that ever-present ghost. All right then, we may say in response to the mirror, we are vile, we know it. Everyone is. That's the way people are. Of course we're like Hitler, and we're sick of lacerating ourselves about it, and as a matter of fact, we're even sick of lacerating Hitler—let him be.

This self-pitying response to the unflattering news that we're not quite good means that we've decided, if that's how things are, that we'll accept evil; we'll no longer make any effort to oppose it. This response leads right towards death.

But it is utterly ridiculous to say that people are vile. If we step outside and pay a brief visit to the nearest supermarket or the nearest café, we will find ourselves in a position to see, scattered perhaps among scenes of ugliness and greed, examples—some number of examples—of behavior which is thoughtful or kind, moments when someone could easily have been cold or cruel but in fact was not. Perhaps we will see the very same person do something harsh and a moment later something gentle. Everyone knows that this element of goodness exists, that it can grow, or that it can die, and there's something particularly disingenuous and cheap about extricating oneself from the human struggle with the whispered excuse that it's already over.

NEW PLAYS

★ **HONOUR by Joanna Murray-Smith.** In a series of intense confrontations, a wife, husband, lover and daughter negotiate the forces of passion, history, responsibility and honour. "HONOUR makes for surprisingly interesting viewing. Tight, crackling dialogue (usually played out in punchy verbal duels) captures characters unable to deal with emotions … Murray-Smith effectively places her characters in situations that strip away pretense." –*Variety* "… the play's virtues are strong: a distinctive theatrical voice, passionate concerns … HONOUR might just capture a few honors of its own." –*Time Out Magazine* [1M, 3W] ISBN: 0-8222-1683-3

★ **MR. PETERS' CONNECTIONS by Arthur Miller.** Mr. Miller describes the protagonist as existing in a dream-like state when the mind is "freed to roam from real memories to conjectures, from trivialities to tragic insights, from terror of death to glorying in one's being alive." With this memory play, the Tony Award and Pulitzer Prize-winner reaffirms his stature as the world's foremost dramatist. "… a cross between Joycean stream-of-consciousness and Strindberg's dream plays, sweetened with a dose of William Saroyan's philosophical whimsy … CONNECTIONS is most intriguing …" –*The NY Times* [5M, 3W] ISBN: 0-8222-1687-6

★ **THE WAITING ROOM by Lisa Loomer.** Three women from different centuries meet in a doctor's waiting room in this dark comedy about the timeless quest for beauty – and its cost. "… THE WAITING ROOM … is a bold, risky melange of conflicting elements that is … terrifically moving … There's no resisting the fierce emotional pull of the play." –*The NY Times* "… one of the high points of this year's Off-Broadway season … THE WAITING ROOM is well worth a visit." –*Back Stage* [7M, 4W, flexible casting] ISBN: 0-8222-1594-2

★ **THE OLD SETTLER by John Henry Redwood.** A sweet-natured comedy about two church-going sisters in 1943 Harlem and the handsome young man who rents a room in their apartment. "For all of its decent sentiments, THE OLD SETTLER avoids sentimentality. It has the authenticity and lack of pretense of an Early American sampler." –*The NY Times* "We've had some fine plays Off-Broadway this season, and this is one of the best." –*The NY Post* [1M, 3W] ISBN: 0-8-222-1642-6

★ **THE LAST TRAIN TO NIBROC by Arlene Hutton.** In 1940 two young strangers share a seat on a train bound east only to find their paths will cross again. "All aboard. LAST TRAIN TO NIBROC is a sweetly told little chamber romance." –*Show Business* "… [a] gently charming little play, reminiscent of Thorton Wilder in its look at rustic Americans who are to be treasured for their simplicity and directness …" –*Associated Press* "The old formula of boy wins girls, boy loses girl, boy wins girl still works … [a] well-made play that perfectly captures a slice of small-town-life-gone-by." –*Back Stage* [1M, 1W] ISBN: 0-8222-1753-8

★ **OVER THE RIVER AND THROUGH THE WOODS by Joe DiPietro.** Nick sees both sets of his grandparents every Sunday for dinner. This is routine until he has to tell them that he's been offered a dream job in Seattle. The news doesn't sit so well. "A hilarious family comedy that is even funnier than his long running musical revue *I Love You, You're Perfect, Now Change.*" –*Back Stage* "Loaded with laughs every step of the way." –*Star-Ledger* [3M, 3W] ISBN: 0-8222-1712-0

★ **SIDE MAN by Warren Leight.** 1999 Tony Award winner. This is the story of a broken family and the decline of jazz as popular entertainment. "… a tender, deeply personal memory play about the turmoil in the family of a jazz musician as his career crumbles at the dawn of the age of rock-and-roll …" –*The NY Times* "[SIDE MAN] is an elegy for two things – a lost world and a lost love. When the two notes sound together in harmony, it is moving and graceful …" –*The NY Daily News* "An atmospheric memory play…with crisp dialogue and clearly drawn characters … reflects the passing of an era with persuasive insight … The joy and despair of the musicians is skillfully illustrated." –*Variety* [5M, 3W] ISBN: 0-8222-1721-X

DRAMATISTS PLAY SERVICE, INC.
440 Park Avenue South, New York, NY 10016 212-683-8960 Fax 212-213-1539
postmaster@dramatists.com   www.dramatists.com

NEW PLAYS

★ **CLOSER by Patrick Marber.** Winner of the 1998 Olivier Award for Best Play and the 1999 New York Drama Critics Circle Award for Best Foreign Play. Four lives intertwine over the course of four and a half years in this densely plotted, stinging look at modern love and betrayal. "CLOSER is a sad, savvy, often funny play that casts a steely, unblinking gaze at the world of relationships and lets you come to your own conclusions ... CLOSER does not merely hold your attention; it burrows into you." –*New York Magazine* "A powerful, darkly funny play about the cosmic collision between the sun of love and the comet of desire." –*Newsweek Magazine* [2M, 2W] ISBN: 0-8222-1722-8

★ **THE MOST FABULOUS STORY EVER TOLD by Paul Rudnick.** A stage manager, headset and prompt book at hand, brings the house lights to half, then dark, and cues the creation of the world. Throughout the play, she's in control of everything. In other words, she's either God, or she thinks she is. "Line by line, Mr. Rudnick may be the funniest writer for the stage in the United States today ... One-liners, epigrams, withering put-downs and flashing repartee: These are the candles that Mr. Rudnick lights instead of cursing the darkness ... a testament to the virtues of laughing ... and in laughter, there is something like the memory of Eden." –*The NY Times* "Funny it is ... consistently, rapaciously, deliriously ... easily the funniest play in town." –*Variety* [4M, 5W] ISBN: 0-8222-1720-1

★ **A DOLL'S HOUSE by Henrik Ibsen, adapted by Frank McGuinness.** Winner of the 1997 Tony Award for Best Revival. "New, raw, gut-twisting and gripping. Easily the hottest drama this season." –*USA Today* "Bold, brilliant and alive." –*The Wall Street Journal* "A thunderclap of an evening that takes your breath away." –*Time Magazine* [4M, 4W, 2 boys] ISBN: 0-8222-1636-1

★ **THE HERBAL BED by Peter Whelan.** The play is based on actual events which occurred in Stratford-upon-Avon in the summer of 1613, when William Shakespeare's elder daughter was publicly accused of having a sexual liaison with a married neighbor and family friend. "In his probing new play, THE HERBAL BED ... Peter Whelan muses about a sidelong event in the life of Shakespeare's family and creates a finely textured tapestry of love and lies in the early 17th-century Stratford." –*The NY Times* "It is a first rate drama with interesting moral issues of truth and expediency." –*The NY Post* [5M, 3W] ISBN: 0-8222-1675-2

★ **SNAKEBIT by David Marshall Grant.** A study of modern friendship when put to the test. "... a rather smart and absorbing evening of water-cooler theater, the intimate sort of Off-Broadway experience that has you picking apart the recognizable characters long after the curtain calls." – *The NY Times* "Off-Broadway keeps on presenting us with compelling reasons for going to the theater. The latest is SNAKEBIT, David Marshall Grant's smart new comic drama about being thirtysomething and losing one's way in life." –*The NY Daily News* [3M, 1W] ISBN: 0-8222-1724-4

★ **A QUESTION OF MERCY by David Rabe.** The Obie Award-winning playwright probes the sensitive and controversial issue of doctor-assisted suicide in the age of AIDS in this poignant drama. "There are many devastating ironies in Mr. Rabe's beautifully considered, piercingly clear-eyed work ..." –*The NY Times* "With unsettling candor and disturbing insight, the play arouses pity and understanding of a troubling subject ... Rabe's provocative tale is an affirmation of dignity that rings clear and true." –*Variety* [6M, 1W] ISBN: 0-8222-1643-4

★ **DIMLY PERCEIVED THREATS TO THE SYSTEM by Jon Klein.** Reality and fantasy overlap with hilarious results as this unforgettable family attempts to survive the nineties. "Here's a play whose point about fractured families goes to the heart, mind – and ears." –*The Washington Post* "... an end-of-the millennium comedy about a family on the verge of a nervous breakdown ... Trenchant and hilarious ..." –*The Baltimore Sun* [2M, 4W] ISBN: 0-8222-1677-9

DRAMATISTS PLAY SERVICE, INC.
440 Park Avenue South, New York, NY 10016 212-683-8960 Fax 212-213-1539
postmaster@dramatists.com www.dramatists.com

NEW PLAYS

★ **AS BEES IN HONEY DROWN by Douglas Carter Beane.** Winner of the John Gassner Playwriting Award. A hot young novelist finds the subject of his new screenplay in a New York socialite who leads him into the world of *Auntie Mame* and *Breakfast at Tiffany's*, before she takes him for a ride. "A delicious soufflé of a satire ... [an] extremely entertaining fable for an age that always chooses image over substance." –*The NY Times* "... A witty assessment of one of the most active and relentless industries in a consumer society ... the creation of 'hot' young things, which the media have learned to mass produce with efficiency and zeal." –*The NY Daily News* [3M, 3W, flexible casting] ISBN: 0-8222-1651-5

★ **STUPID KIDS by John C. Russell.** In rapid, highly stylized scenes, the story follows four high-school students as they make their way from first through eighth period and beyond, struggling with the fears, frustrations, and longings peculiar to youth. "In STUPID KIDS ... playwright John C. Russell gets the opera of adolescence to a T ... The stylized teenspeak of STUPID KIDS ... suggests that Mr. Russell may have hidden a tape recorder under a desk in study hall somewhere and then scoured the tapes for good quotations ... it is the kids' insular, ceaselessly churning world, a pre-adult world of Doritos and libidos, that the playwright seeks to lay bare." –*The NY Times* "STUPID KIDS [is] a sharp-edged ... whoosh of teen angst and conformity anguish. It is also very funny." –*NY Newsday* [2M, 2W] ISBN: 0-8222-1698-1

★ **COLLECTED STORIES by Donald Margulies.** From Obie Award-winner Donald Margulies comes a provocative analysis of a student-teacher relationship that turns sour when the protégé becomes a rival. "With his fine ear for detail, Margulies creates an authentic, insular world, and he gives equal weight to the opposing viewpoints of two formidable characters." –*The LA Times* "This is probably Margulies' best play to date ..." –*The NY Post* "... always fluid and lively, the play is thick with ideas, like a stock-pot of good stew." –*The Village Voice* [2W] ISBN: 0-8222-1640-X

★ **FREEDOMLAND by Amy Freed.** An overdue showdown between a son and his father sets off fireworks that illuminate the neurosis, rage and anxiety of one family – and of America at the turn of the millennium. "FREEDOMLAND's more obvious links are to *Buried Child* and *Bosoms and Neglect*. Freed, like Guare, is an inspired wordsmith with a gift for surreal touches in situations grounded in familiar and real territory." –*Curtain Up* [3M, 4W] ISBN: 0-8222-1719-8

★ **STOP KISS by Diana Son.** A poignant and funny play about the ways, both sudden and slow, that lives can change irrevocably. "There's so much that is vital and exciting about STOP KISS ... you want to embrace this young author and cheer her onto other works ... the writing on display here is funny and credible ... you also will be charmed by its heartfelt characters and up-to-the-minute humor." –*The NY Daily News* "... irresistibly exciting ... a sweet, sad, and enchantingly sincere play." –*The NY Times* [3M, 3W] ISBN: 0-8222-1731-7

★ **THREE DAYS OF RAIN by Richard Greenberg.** The sins of fathers and mothers make for a bittersweet elegy in this poignant and revealing drama. "... a work so perfectly judged it heralds the arrival of a major playwright ... Greenberg is extraordinary." –*The NY Daily News* "Greenberg's play is filled with graceful passages that are by turns melancholy, harrowing, and often, quite funny." –*Variety* [2M, 1W] ISBN: 0-8222-1676-0

★ **THE WEIR by Conor McPherson.** In a bar in rural Ireland, the local men swap spooky stories in an attempt to impress a young woman from Dublin who recently moved into a nearby "haunted" house. However, the tables are soon turned when she spins a yarn of her own. "You shed all sense of time at this beautiful and devious new play." –*The NY Times* "Sheer theatrical magic. I have rarely been so convinced that I have just seen a modern classic. Tremendous." –*The London Daily Telegraph* [4M, 1W] ISBN: 0-8222-1706-6

DRAMATISTS PLAY SERVICE, INC.
440 Park Avenue South, New York, NY 10016 212-683-8960 Fax 212-213-1539
postmaster@dramatists.com www.dramatists.com